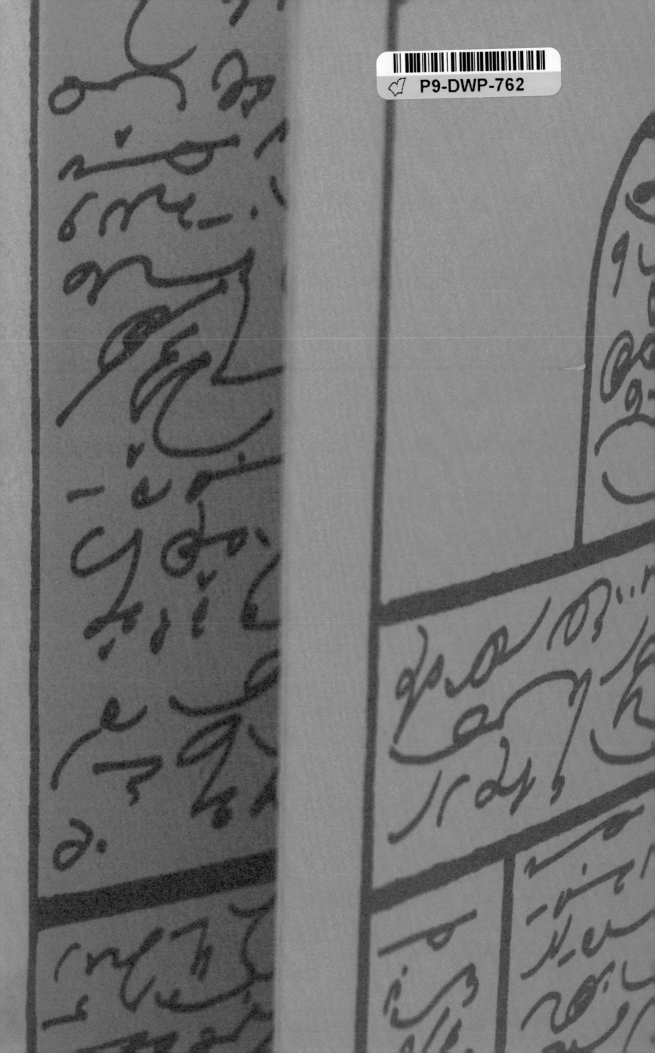

HAND, VOICE, & VISION:

ARTISTS' BOOKS FROM WOMEN'S STUDIO WORKSHOP

CURATED BY KATHLEEN WALKUP

HAND, VOICE, & VISION: Artists' Books from Women's Studio Workshop is a traveling exhibition. For more information about hosting *HAND, VOICE, VISION*, please visit www.handvoicevision.com.

The Grolier Club, New York, NY
DECEMBER 8, 2010 – FEBRUARY 5, 2011

University of Southern Maine
SPRING 2011

Smith College
FALL 2011

Vassar College
SPRING 2012

Carleton College
FALL 2012

Scripps College
WINTER 2013

© 2010 WOMEN'S STUDIO WORKSHOP
ISBN: 1-893125-78-5

General editor: Kathleen Walkup
Copy editor: Elizabeth Jenson
Catalogue design: Dawn McCusker
Exhibition design: Elizabeth Fischbach
Additional design: Dawn McCusker
Catalogue typography: Goudy Old Style and Meta
Printing: Lithography by Design, Highland, NY

CONTENTS

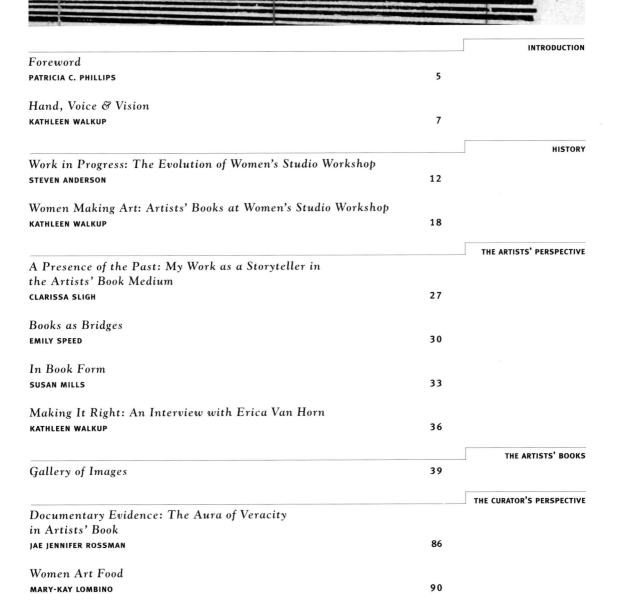

FOREWORD

Books are evocative prompts that summon somatic, embodied engagement to address **PATRICIA C. PHILLIPS** striking perceptual and intellectual experience of form and content. Who hasn't sought to sequester oneself in devouring privacy to hold, read, and dwell with a book? And who hasn't, just as eagerly, sought to share a special or provocative book with a friend or group of students? In their most prosaic and eccentric forms, books are complex surrogates and reliable representatives—of the human condition.

Fortunately, for those of us who desire all imaginable kinds and forms of books there are artists who make exquisitely bracing books. Sometimes artists make books independently, but many seek and require facilities, residencies, and communities to produce a book. There are a handful of places that have become the legendary, sometimes idiosyncratic, and independently enterprising site of artists' book production in the late 20th century. A selected list of past and ongoing spaces includes the Visual Studies Workshop, Franklin Furnace, Printed Matter, Nexus Press, the Woman's Building (all in the United States), Nova Scotia College of Art and Design, Bookworks (London), and Art Metropole (Toronto).

Founded by four artists, Barbara Leoff Burge, Ann Kalmbach, Tatana Kellner, and Anita Wetzel, in 1974, the Women's Studio Workshop is one of the most distinctive and persistent sites for the production and preservation of artists' books. In 1979, it officially began its book publishing program and since its relocation in Binnewater Lane in the small town of Rosendale, New York, in 1983, WSW has been a temporary home for hundreds of artists to make books, frequently side-by-side with other independent artists, in the organization's elegantly simple "fresh air" facilities.

Artists are invited to work at the Women's Studio Workshop through a juried process. This commitment to seek and represent a broad spectrum of multiple views creates and perpetuates an expansive cultural perspective within the Women's Studio Workshop's progressive, energetic organization. The collection of books produced (and there are more than 180 as of this writing, with five added each year) represents an exceptional range of forms and processes, pressing issues, and individual positions. As a collection, these books make tangible more than thirty years of cultural, social, political, and theoretical developments.

In her essay, " Critical Metalanguage for the Artist's Book" (1995), Johanna Drucker pursues an internal debate between personal reflections and critical analysis on the shifting character and multiple dimensions of the artist's book. The initial dialectical call and response slowly merges into a flowing current of ideas of emotional and intellectual depth. At the denouement of the essay, Drucker's "two" voices enfold in a subtle but intricate singularity. In many respects, her brilliant essay models how the frequently complex components of a book coalesce into a coherent object.

The following are several examples of artists' books—and artists' preoccupations. Clarissa Sligh's *Wrongly Bodied Two* (2004) is an eloquently unfolding dialogic examination of boundary crossings, transition, and identity. The book includes references to Ellen Craft, a nineteenth century slave from Georgia who disguised herself as a white gentleman slave-owner in order to smuggle herself and her husband across the Mason-Dixon Line. In a wildly promiscuous display of posturing and impersonation, she moved from black to white, slave to owner, woman to man, and wife to master, her vivid story serving as a prescient narrative touchstone to the four-year sexual transition of Deborah to Jake McBee.

In another visually layered narrative, Marisol Limon Martinez rescues partially formed recollections of her grandmother Amelia Quinones Gonzales (1898 – 1990). Born in Torreón, Coahuila, Mexico, all of her personal family documents were destroyed by fire during the Mexican Revolution. The artist's book *Forgotten Knowledge* (2002) explores her grandmother—the incineration of her identity and the rich character of her long life—shortly after the artist's own studio was destroyed by fire.

In 1997, WSW founders Ann Kalmbach and Tatana Kellner made *Pistol/Pistil: botanical ballistics* to examine both the rhetorical and opportunistic merger of militarization and agrarian/agricultural traditions. Interrogating the book and language through a sleight-of-hand process of withholding, Heidi Neilson's *Atlas of Punctuation* (2004) withdraws all of the words from passages by Virginia Woolf, Italo Calvino, Dr. Seuss, and Jorge Luis Borges, leaving stunningly cryptic "texts" of residual commas, periods, and end of sentence punctuation.

PATRICIA C. PHILLIPS IS AN INDEPENDENT WRITER AND (SOMETIMES) CURATOR OF ART, DESIGN, AND PUBLIC ART. SHE IS DEAN OF GRADUATE STUDIES AT RHODE ISLAND SCHOOL OF DESIGN.

The artists' books represented in this exhibition (many of which I had the pleasure to hold and read during a quiet Sunday afternoon one April at the Women's Studio Workshop) offer vivid evidence of the pleasures and challenges of engaging a magnitude of form and content, as well as WSW's prodigious and persistent commitment to provide and consistently renew a critical, yet supportive, space for cultural production. We see neither a "WSW style" nor commonly held sensibility, but a collection/representation of artists' capacity to intervene in a traditional form and reinvent and recalibrate its conditions through the imaginative application of materials and methodologies guided by aesthetic and intellectual preoccupations. To dwell with these generous and stimulating books, we palpably experience the dynamic, complex culture we share in common.

HAND, VOICE & VISION

In 1979, Women's Studio Workshop inaugurated its publishing program for the **KATHLEEN WALKUP** production and distribution of handmade artists' books. The term artist's book, used to describe a genre of creative work that focused on the book as a material object, had been in general use for less than ten years when the program began. This new art form was fed variously by conceptual art, attempts to move art away from the traditional gallery system, the advent of conservators interested in studying the underlying structure of the book, and by a younger generation of private press publishers who were printing new rather than classic texts using traditional technologies. These seemingly disparate threads were woven into something new, books that were art as opposed to books that catalogued and described art. To this mix the four founders of Women's Studio Workshop—Barbara Leoff Burge, Ann Kalmbach, Tatana Kellner, and Anita Wetzel—added their collective goal to be recognized both as artists and as women who were making art.

More than thirty years later, WSW is the largest publisher of handmade artists' books in the U.S. Each one of the books has been chosen from artists' proposals submitted to an outside jury, which itself changes each year. This democratic approach has resulted in a rich mix of books by women (and a few men) that are diverse in form, technique, and content.

Access to a broad array of techniques for the production of editioned works was a key issue for the founders of WSW. Purchase and renovation of the Binnewater Arts Center in Rosendale, New York, in 1983, allowed WSW to develop studios in the areas of letterpress, screen-printing, etching, papermaking, photography, and ceramics. These techniques have afforded artists the opportunity for broad exploration and experimentation while making their books. Classes and workshops, a studio manager, instructors, and interns provide further assistance and support.

This exhibition, which celebrates more than thirty years of artists' book publications at the Women's Studio Workshop, recognizes three inter-related facets that together characterize the strength of the artists' books published by the Workshop.

HAND represents the mark of the maker in the books. The artists chosen to be in residence at the Workshop bring their practice as hands-on artists to the experience.

This making of art has been fundamental to the WSW experience since the first days when the four founders worked in their house cum studio on a tree-lined street in Rosendale.

Deborah Frederick's *Eight Breakfasts in 8 Pages* in many ways epitomizes the WSW artmaking experience; on its surface it appears to celebrate the quotidian act of sitting in a local café with a morning muffin, a book, or a friend, but Frederick's underlying impulse was to develop a project that would force her to draw every day. By choosing a public place in which to do this she suggests that artmaking is both an individual discipline and a collective act. Heather O'Hara's energetic examination of global politics, *The Handbook of Practical Geographies*, has woodcut images that spill out of the page borders in a tour de force of handwork in the aid of tongue-in-cheek political "lessons". *Skim Milk & Soft Wax* is Dani Leventhal's exploration of her identity. The book uses digital printing, silkscreen, drypoint, drawing, a three-dimensional object on the cover, and a DVD, an interwoven set of materials that echo the complexity of reconciling contemporary Jewish identity with troubling Israeli policies.

VOICE acknowledges some of the recurring themes that have been addressed in the books over the years. While the books reflect diverse viewpoints, certain general motifs appear with some regularity. Personal and cultural narrative, self-image, and political observation are all themes that have found resonance with WSW resident artists. Artists have also created conceptually based work, and more than one has interrogated the form of the artist's book.

Don't Bug the Waitress is Susan Baker's amusing and pointed exposé of the wait trade. It is one of many food-related books in WSW's collection. Marisol Limon Martinez' book of personal memory, *Forgotten Knowledge*, explores family, home, and loss in an evocation of the artist's great-grandmother. Family and domesticity are unsurprising topics of many WSW books, but the power of individual voices such as that of Martinez to evoke deeper meaning in these daily concerns provides readers with the possibility of new insights into standard themes.

VISION celebrates the extraordinary work of artists whose ideas and execution have transcended everyday practice to suggest new directions for the medium of artists' books. Artists like Sharon Gilbert, Erica Van Horn, and Susan King (whose *Women and Cars* is represented in Voice) were both early and ongoing practitioners of artists' bookmaking. Gilbert, who died in 2005, contributed many works to the archive of early artists' books. King and Van Horn continue their activity; both have studios well outside urban settings and both include books as part but not all of their practice. Clarissa Sligh's visionary work has had a singular impact on the field of contemporary artists' books. She is one of a select group of artists who have completed more than one book at WSW. Heidi Neilson and Maureen Cummins are among the younger artists whose work is shifting the conversation about what an artist's book can be. In Neilson's *Atlas of Punctuation*, the use of letterpress production ironically shifts the conceptual content of her book into the twenty-first century and away from offset-printed multiples of the 1970s. Cummins' superbly produced *The Business is Suffering* juxtaposes lush trappings of traditional bookmaking (half leather binding, moldmade paper, letterpress, and silkscreen printing) with letters written by nineteenth-century slave owners detailing the often highly personal ways in which they commodified African-Americans as chattel.

The word vision most aptly applies to the four founders themselves, whose prescience about the potential for the medium of artists' books in the 1970s has led to this extraordinary body of work. While all four of the artists have produced work for the collection, it is Ann Kalmbach and Tatana Kellner's work, often in collaboration, that has formed the backbone of WSW's artists' book publications since the first book, produced by Kellner, in 1979. In this exhibition Kalmbach and Kellner are represented by four collaborations that represent three time periods in WSW's publication history. *Headdress*, made in 1983, is one of their earliest collaborative works, an image-only book that amusingly explores the dictum that form follows function. *Pistol, Pistil: botanical ballistics* (1997) represents the continuing political interests of Kalmbach and Kellner. *Errors of the Amanuensis* and *Transatlantic Balderdash* (both 2010) are interrelated books completed at a residency in Germany, both commenting on the vicissitudes of language, another enduring interest.

Finally, Kellner's own significant and ongoing contributions to WSW's collection are represented by two works (*71125: Fifty Years of Silence, Eva Kellner's Story* and *B-11226: Fifty Years of Silence, Eugene Kellner's Story*) that honor her Czech parents. Each of the wooden boxed books holds a mold of one parent's arm showing the tattooed numbers given to them when they were taken to the concentration camps during World War II. Both parents survived the camps; Kellner tells their stories through their, personal recollections, and family photographs. These two books, with a combination of materiality, process, and intensely personal content, serve as representatives of the best that the publications of WSW have to offer; it is not surprising that they serve as the most iconic works not only in Kellner's own production, but that of the Women's Studio Workshop's artists' book program itself.

Curating this exhibition has been a privilege and a wonderful opportunity to thoroughly explore the publications of Women's Studio Workshop, which have added so significantly to the canon of artists' books in the United States. I am deeply

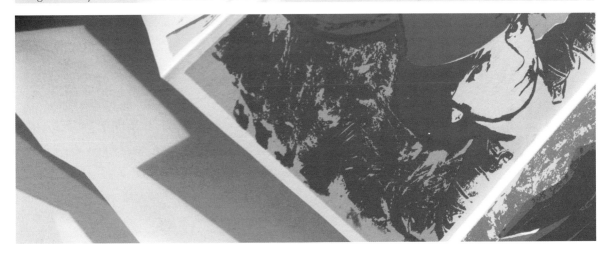

indebted to the founders of WSW for granting me this honor, and to my former student and now WSW Office Manager Sandra Brown, who has never failed to be helpful throughout this work. Anita Wetzel has been invaluable in arranging funding, overseeing details, and providing professional and personal support, including airport rides. Thanks to Chris Petrone for managing to arrange my stays in what has come to seem like my own personal apartment, and to intern Lindsay Gleason for her careful work with the archive and her help with choosing books for the exhibition.

Thanks, too, to all of the catalogue essayists, whose thoughtful and learned contributions will insure that the catalogue has a life well beyond this exhibition.

Two Elizabeths have been steady, invaluable, and invariably supportive throughout the process of pulling together both the exhibition and the catalogue. Elizabeth Jensen, editor extraordinaire, rescued the catalogue time and again with her thorough and thoughtful editing. Elizabeth Fischbach's incredible knowledge and evidently bottomless energy meant that the exhibition design would be highly integrated, professional, and lively; it is impossible to overstate her contributions to the physical and aesthetic integrity of the exhibition.

Thanks to Eric Holzenberg and Megan Smith at the Grolier Club, who kept us on track with the exhibition, and to Robert Ruben, who not only suggested this exhibition and fostered the proposal through several drafts until it reflected the level of attention that the Grolier Club deserves, but also provided a model through his own stellar exhibition and catalogue of artists' books from his personal collection.

At Mills College, support from Special Collections Librarian Janice Braun meant that my students could spend countless hours in the Heller Rare Book Room studying and discussing WSW books. Thanks to my students in my artists' books seminars for providing thoughtful analyses and interesting writing about these books.

In Ireland, where I was lucky enough to spend time while writing and editing the catalogue, Erica Van Horn and Simon Cutts gave me shelter, food, no end of books to read, and a calm retreat at what seemed like the edge of the world; I am very grateful for their friendship and their trust. Thanks also to Susan King for always being willing to read, correct, amend, and support my writing on the subject of women and artists' books.

Most importantly, I want to thank Ann and Tana profusely for their dedication to the project and their faith in my ability to see it to fruition. They opened their home to me, fed me, and made sure I got out from behind the computer and spent time in the clean air of the Rosendale countryside. An exhibition and catalogue of this scale are daunting undertakings for all involved. The fact that Ann, Tana, and the rest of the women at WSW trusted me to have my own vision about sharing their work with the public has made this work highly rewarding, and I am grateful to them for doing so.

Kathleen Walkup is Professor of Book Art and Director of the Book Art Program at Mills College, where she teaches typography and letterpress printing, artists' bookmaking and seminar/studio courses that combine print culture and book history with studio projects. She is also Book Art Director for the MFA in Book Art & Creative Writing, the first such program in the country. Walkup's interests include the history of women in print culture and conceptual practice in artists' books; she has lectured and written widely on these areas. Hand, Voice & Vision: Artists' Books from Women's Studio Workshop (Grolier Club, New York, 2010, plus several other venues) is her most recent curatorial project. In 2008 she curated Mutanabbi Street starts here, an international gathering of broadsides in response to the bombing of booksellers' row in Baghdad. Her installation [re]Covering the Jungle was part of the invitational exhibition Banned & Recovered: Artists respond to censorship at the African American Museum in Oakland, California, 2008. The work is part of her ongoing project, Library of Discards.

Walkup is co-founder and Executive Vice President of College Book Art Association. She has taught in Stanford University's Continuing Studies Program as well as at Camberwell College of Art, London, and the University of Georgia's Lamar Dodd School of Art Studies Abroad Program in Cortona, Italy. She is a consultant for the PBS program Craft in America, and writes a seasonal blog, New Irish Journal.

WORK IN PROGRESS:

THE EVOLUTION OF WOMEN'S STUDIO WORKSHOP

STEVEN ANDERSEN On a brilliant May afternoon, a bluebird day, a pleasant breeze filters through the second floor of the Women's Studio Workshop. The silkscreen studio is an assembly line of sorts today, with cardboard and paper staged along a long sequence of tables. Tona Wilson, a resident artist, with the help of interns and volunteers is constructing the case for her book, a four-volume document of her work as a Spanish interpreter in the prison and court systems.

Her two-month residency is already over, but the book still isn't done—not an uncommon occurrence. The work goes on, as it will for another month, until the project is complete. Such overruns are an inevitable part of the game, drawing occasional grumbles from the staff, but accommodated nonetheless. Creating an artist's book is a complicated, involved process, and it's the rare artist who completes an ambitious project ahead of schedule.

That kind of flexibility is typical of the Workshop, where it seems everyone makes daily compromises to keep the institution and its many programs moving forward and growing, but it's not the only thing that sets it apart.

The Women's Studio Workshop provides the only visual arts residency program in the world dedicated exclusively to women, who remain absurdly underrepresented in the art world. It's the largest publisher of hand printed artists' books in the country, and with the sustainable fibers grown on its ArtFarm can produce books from seed to binding in-house. It's also notable for its accessibility, DIY ethic, and utter lack of pretension.

Perhaps the Workshop's most significant quality, however, is a rare continuity that enables it to grow organically and remain true to its core vision. All the best intentions would matter little if the organization did not survive. But from the beginning, the Women's Studio Workshop has steadily grown and expanded its scope. After thirty-six years, the institution's four founders are still running the show, on good terms, and looking to the future.

Sitting in the tall front windows of the Workshop on this sunny Thursday, Barbara Leoff Burge recalls the Workshop's early days. Babs is gregarious and engaging, with a keen eye and a quick wit. Although she's never been involved in the day-to-day operations as much as the other founders, throughout the WSW's history she's been on hand to take on random tasks, teach, and do design work. Her current role as a member of the board of directors makes good use of her sociability—she's a natural ambassador. But at the outset, it was her role as a mentor that was critical.

Babs is seventeen years older than the other three founders—she's 76, though you'd never guess it—and her frustrating experiences as a young artist and teacher did a lot to shape the Workshop.

"It was a guys' scene—art school [The School of the Art Institute of Chicago] was, and the art world pretty much was, too," she says. "I was hired as an art teacher at Dutchess Community College, and they said, 'We don't really want to hire you, no matter what your qualifications are, because we don't want a woman teaching fine art. But if you agree under those circumstances, then you can teach.' What could I do? I needed a job."

"I busted my hump. I really did. I even wrote a little textbook. Of course, they ended up letting me go, telling me what a good job I did. I think I had a little bit of breakdown."

She was angry and upset, and was ready, she says, to do something for women, when one day she noticed two college students poking around her driveway.

Ann Kalmbach and Anita Wetzel met each other singing in the New Paltz choir. They lived in the same dorm, were both in the art department, and became fast friends. When Ken Burge, one of Ann's instructors, showed them his wife's drawings one day, something struck a chord.

"Kenny used to bring my drawings to class and say, 'These belong to Barbara Burge; she's not my sister and she's not my mother,'" Babs says, laughing.

The drawings made such an impression that Anita and Ann decided to seek out the artist.

"When we saw her work, it just blew my mind," Anita says. "I couldn't believe this person lived right here in New Paltz. She really was a role model."

The three artists started drawing together, often drawing each other. It was their first time working in a group outside the unapologetically male-dominated art-school world, and it was a revelation.

"When we started working with Barbara it was just a really different experience than being in school," Ann recalls. "It was more collegial and less competitive, and that seemed like a valuable model. We were really unaware of it existing out in the other world."

When Ann and Anita graduated, the collaboration went on hiatus for a couple of years. Ann departed for the MFA program at the Rochester Institute of Technology, though Babs served as her advisor. Anita traveled after graduating, but settled back in the New Paltz area. When Ann returned from grad school with a new partner, Tatana Kellner, in tow, the group dynamic took a new shape and an unlikely plan was forged.

"I don't know how, but I heard about this grant, a State Council on the Arts grant," Anita says. "I just wrote this thing out and then forgot all about it. Then one day I got a phone call saying, 'We're coming to see you tomorrow.' I was like, what?"

At the time, 1974, an arts organization didn't need to be up and running to qualify for a grant in New York, and the incipient group's plan was simple, to create a printmaking studio. There was a clear need—SUNY had no cogent printmaking technology at the time, and there was no organized instruction available in the region. Still, winning the grant came as a surprise.

The money was a trifle, just $2,100, but the four artists pooled their equipment and supplies, rented a house on James Street in Rosendale—a lot cheaper than New Paltz—and set up shop as the Women's Studio Collective. Their sympathetic landlord didn't mind the presses, screens, and washbasins they installed, and before long a working studio took shape.

The initial mission was straightforward—public access art instruction—but a gradual evolution soon began that lead to a constantly expanding range of efforts and initiatives. They started making paper in the attic, and launched an off-site film and video series. After about five years, the founders, who initially had to keep side jobs, actually started getting paid and it became apparent that their little collective was turning into something much bigger.

In 1979, the organization, now called the Women's Studio Workshop, purchased its first property on Binnewater Road, a mile north of Main Street Rosendale. The nineteenth century building was originally the general store for the Rosendale Cement Co., and most recently had been a bait-and-tackle shop. It took three years to renovate it into a studio and build an addition that nearly doubled the space.

"When we got to the point of buying a building, we realized this was bigger than any of us," Ann says. "Bear in mind the building was $16,000 dollars. But it still was the biggest check that I've ever written."

Other buildings followed, three in all (acquisition of a fourth is pending), and with them the capacity for a full residency program, clay and letterpress studios, and expanded education programs. Ann was instrumental in getting the neighborhood certified as the Binnewater Historic District, adding another facet—historic preservation—to the WSW mission.

The fruition of that $2,100 seed is astounding, but it has taken a lot more than money for the Women's Studio Workshop to become the institution it is today.

From the beginning, each of the founders gravitated to specific, and complementary, roles in the organization. Anita can trace the circuitous path to her current title of development director to drafting that first grant application.

"She's really the quietest person of all four of us—quiet and reserved and ladylike," Babs says. "She just goes about her business and writes the grants. Sometimes the deadlines are hanging over her head and she's just deep into the computer. There's a lot of noise all around—phones ringing and dogs barking and children crying—and she's able to get it done."

Not that it's easy. In fact, the frenetic early days of the Workshop took their toll on Anita, leaving her exhausted by 1980. She needed a break. To escape frantic country life she moved to the halcyon confines of New York City, where she spent the next fourteen years working part time and making art. But the charms of the Binne ultimately lured her back.

"I definitely burned out," she says. "It was a 24/7 thing. When I came back I knew how to take care of myself. I knew my parameters were different."

Anita, who is tall and thin, and generally wears a curious smile, is a decided contrast to Ann, the executive director. Ann's default expression is of furrowed brow, and can come off gruff on first impression. That countenance, however, belies her dry humor and a natural executive's ease with authority.

"Nobody knows as much about the workings of the Workshop as Ann does," Babs says. "She's the one with the vision for the future."Watching Ann in the WSW office over the course of a day, one can't help notice her even keel. She shifts among the various aspects of the Workshop's operations—fundraising to facilities issues, resident artists to real estate—without the subtlest hitch. She makes decisions swiftly, but can change her mind without hesitation if someone presents a better case, and she always has one eye on the horizon, looking for the next opportunity.

"Ann isn't afraid to watch over the whole thing," Anita says, "and also—with the real estate stuff, for example—to just be creative."

But if Ann is the organizational mind of the WSW, it's Tana who is the relentless creative force. It's easy to overlook Tana when first visiting the Workshop. She is small and quiet and works in a little side office, often by herself. But any assumptions are dispelled the moment she engages you with her intent, observant eyes.

Tana speaks softly, and her accent tends to draw one even closer, to pay more careful attention. Then come her thoughtful, direct questions—questions that can make you instantly wonder just how thoroughly you've thought things through. It's this quiet intensity and intellectual rigor that fuels the studio programs, and keeps artists on track.

Tana's family escaped the Iron Curtain at the end of Prague Spring, the brief period of liberalization in 1968 when Czechoslovakians were free to travel west. Her parents, Holocaust survivors, settled the family in Toledo, Ohio.

"Have you ever been to Toledo?" she asks. "Then you can imagine how exciting it was after Prague. I tried to get out of there as fast as I could."

Perhaps that legacy of escape—from genocide, from totalitarian oppression, even from the monotony of Ohio—gives Tana her acuteness and vigor. "Tana," Babs says, "has the energy to run the Grand Coulee Dam." In addition to her role as artistic director—she manages the residency and fellowship program, and promotes the sale of artists' books—she has remained the most active artist of the four founders. Most days find her shuttling between that cramped side office and her impressively large studio in a yellow barn across the street, with very little escaping her attention in transit.

The alchemy in the combination of these four personalities has proved potent, balanced, and enduring over the years. "We all have different things," Tana says. "Barbara likes to chat. Anita is more inward and can sort of analyze things. Ann is the idea person. She likes to think forward. She would buy all the buildings she can, given the chance. And I'm much more practical, like, "How are we gonna pay that bill?" So it's a combination of all of these competing forces that made us, and we're still here."

There was never a single vision for what the Women's Studio Workshop would become, and there still isn't. Each founder had her own ideas, some of which came to pass.

Anita initially envisioned a communal live/work space with artistic activity and intellectual rapport. "I think I saw it as a more esoteric thing than what happened," she says. "You know, a salon-type thing; dialogue, critique, work together."

That didn't happen out of the gate. The practical aspects of setting up a studio and bringing in funding took precedence in the early days. But as Tana started going on artist residencies herself in the mid-1980s, the organization shifted its focus from local arts education to hosting residents from across the country and around the world. Today the Workshop offers residents, fellows, and interns a communal experience akin to what Anita dreamed of more than thirty years ago.

Ann, ever the blue-sky thinker, still has a list of programs she'd like to start. "I've toyed a lot with the idea of creating a Masters program," she says. "The internship program is really significant, and it would be interesting to have maybe six students working alongside artists in residence. I've always wanted to do sort of a gallery/frame shop operation, a low-cost, make-it-yourself space. One scheme I was interested in last year was trying to take over the Catholic school to turn it into studios and Art-In-Ed space."

Of course all that takes money, and even funding existing programs in the current economy is a challenge. "Finding money's hard, and it's harder right now," Ann says. "Some of the places we used to get good money from consistently have just dried up. New York state money is going to be way hard—the governor just called for forty percent cuts. Whoa. And it's not like there are new foundations starting up. There's also the element that—though I find it hard to believe—it seems that we're moving into a really conservative kind of time."

This is also a pivotal time for the Workshop. Despite its history of success and ambitious plans, the institution is preparing for what may be its greatest challenge to date. After defying all odds to maintain their collective effort and friendship for nearly four decades, the founders face the prospect of retirement, or at least passing over control of the Workshop to others in the coming years.

This will be particularly hard for Ann and Tana, who have been a couple since the outset, and who live in a house right across the street from the Workshop. Tana, with her practical bent, is clear-eyed and blunt when discussing the difficulty of planning for succession in an organization that has never followed a linear course.

"It's uncharted territory," she says, "and we always do things the hardest way possible, it seems to me. From old buildings, which are not the most suitable studios, to always trying to be independent and do stuff our own way. The challenge is going to be finding the right person. I know from other organizations that the transition is rough. Sometimes the first person doesn't work out. It'll be hard for anybody, because we have been here for such a long time."

On an unseasonably cold, rainy June evening, the Workshop is hosting one of its frequent Friendraisers—events geared to expand the network and awareness of the institution, and hopefully raise some money in the process. Maybe it's the weather, but just three guests show up.

So many interns, staff and board members have come, however, that the guests have no idea they're so few in number—outnumbered, as it turns out, five-to-one. They all get front-row seats to the "Ann & Tana Show," an engaging presentation of artists' books the pair has performed countless times. The effort proves worthwhile. By the end of the evening one guest is interested in taking a class, another in joining the board of directors.

As the interns sweep up downstairs, the founders, along with a few other members of the staff, head back up to the office. No one spends much grief over the small turnout, and the conversation quickly turns to other upcoming fundraising events. There's no time to be disappointed. There's a lot of work to do.

STEVEN ANDERSEN, A WRITER AND ARTIST, LIVES IN ROSENDALE, NEW YORK. HE SERVES ON THE BOARD OF DIRECTORS OF THE WOMEN'S STUDIO WORKSHOP.

WOMEN MAKING ART:

ARTISTS' BOOKS AT WOMEN'S STUDIO WORKSHOP

KATHLEEN WALKUP Every weekday at 12:30 the long plank table in the Women's Studio Workshop office begins to fill up with food. The dishes seem to appear by sleight of hand; what starts out looking like sparse offerings of left-overs soon expands to bounty, and just as magically, people suddenly begin to appear also, as if they have been teleported from their various work spaces tucked into the meandering old building, grabbing plates and piling them high with black beans, tempeh, broken bits of cookie, spaghetti with pesto, beet and carrot salad. Most of the women gathering at the table have been working in the studios since early morning, and they are hungry. They have been pulling heavy paper molds out of vats on the first floor, throwing pots in the basement, lifting silkscreen frames over and over in the second floor studio, running the platen press in the closet-sized room behind the printmaking studio. Everyone finds a spot to hunker down, conversations take place, announcements are made, questions are asked. ("What celebrity would you most like to have associated with the Workshop?") Then just as suddenly lunch is over and everyone disappears back to her work. This quotidian scene is remarkable for one reason: It has been going on for more than thirty-five years.

In 1974, when these potluck lunches began, they were prompted by another type of hunger. Barbara Leoff Burge, Ann Kalmbach, Tatana Kellner, and Anita Wetzel came together to form a new organization simply because they wanted to make art. The litany of reasons why this was so problematic at that time is by now familiar (the original edition of Janson's *History of Art* did not contain a single woman artist, the Metropolitan Museum of Art and the National Gallery of Art had mounted fewer than five solo exhibitions by women artists in the combined 138 years of their existence, less than five percent of all artists represented at the Met were women), but in the 1970s these statistics had a chilling effect on the ability of women to even define themselves as artists, let alone think about how to make or market their art.

The four women, who had settled in the village of Rosendale, New York, about two hours north of New York City, silkscreened t-shirts with the name Women's Studio Collective and began to offer classes in printmaking, painting, and collage in the house where three of them lived. They got their picture in the local newspapers, which described not only the classes but also these living arrangements, pointing out that the "unmarried" women (that is, all but Leoff Burge) lived alongside the studios in their premises on James Street. The popularity of the classes soon meant that the three had to move to new quarters to make room for the attic-to-basement studio. When they moved to a bright yellow building next door to the James Street house Kalmbach had some emotional moments over her concern about the growing scope of their endeavors. In creating this working space the four women were inadvertently joining an ad hoc DIY art movement that included many disenfranchised artists—women, people of color, artists whose work at the edges of mainstream art were not seen as acceptable by the conventional gallery and museum world. By 1974 the historian and critic Lucy Lippard's essay on dematerialized art was a well-known if controversial addition to the art criticism canon. Fluxus and its happenings were in full force. (Dick Higgins, who coined the term intermedia, and Alison Knowles, his partner, both at the center of Fluxus and conceptual art, would later support WSW through three small grants issued by Higgins' mother's foundation.)

On the West Coast the Free Speech Movement begun on the University of California Berkeley campus had helped to awaken in the college generation the realization that marginalized voices could be heard, given the right sort of insistence; this had been most pointedly directed against the ongoing atrocities in Vietnam. (Of course the earlier lessons of civil rights activism, while not always acknowledged, were critical to this understanding.) All across the country, the movement that would come to be called second-wave feminism was becoming an increasingly visible presence not only in marches and demonstrations but on the covers of mainstream magazines like *Time*, where Susan Brownmiller was declared Woman of the Year in 1975 for her passionate writing about rape in *Against Our Will*, and even on the tennis courts, where Billie Jean King defeated the over-confident Bobby Riggs in The Battle of the Sexes. More serious battles were being won in the legislature and the courts, none more critical than *Roe v. Wade*, decided by the Supreme Court in 1973, which gave women legal control over their own bodies for the first time.

For women who simply wanted to make art or to write, the changing political will did not necessarily translate into immediate opportunity. In 1974 the four women who called themselves the Women's Studio Collective did what many women across the country were also doing: create their own physical and, more importantly, mental and emotional spaces in which to do their work.

In the rural spaces of the Lower Hudson Valley where they were living, Leoff Burge, Kalmbach, Kellner, and Wetzel were also moving through the process of building an institution, one that required a new vision away from mainstream models. Wetzel referred to herself and her three co-founders as art desperados. What she meant was that the four women understood the paucity of their chances in the mainstream art world; why not be art outlaws instead? At the James Street house the new vision included etching and intaglio in the living room, stone and plate lithography in the dining room, silkscreen in the basement, and photography in an upstairs bedroom (all of the print washing was done in the bathroom across the hall). Offset was added next; a copy camera was the first piece of equipment purchased from donated funds. Letterpress and ceramics would come later. While their initial interests did not include the new medium of artists' books, their focus on production and particularly on techniques that promoted editions was leading them in the direction of this developing medium.

The women were also experimenting with scale, materials, and production methods, including the re-purposing of "women's" tools toward new ends. For an exhibition in a converted choir loft in a former church in the town of Rhinebeck, New York, the women wanted large pieces that would fill the space. At the same time they were intent on having the work be collaborative, not individual; the spirit of the collective was strong. Finally, the work needed to be inexpensively produced. To make the prints they dipped brooms and mops in ink and drew to scale on bond paper. They then took the artwork to a service bureau that made blue- and red-prints. This method of printing allowed them to hang and drape the four-foot-wide images so they could be seen from the gallery floor below. Since the pieces were only to be used for one exhibition the ephemerality of the substrate was not a concern. This type of experimentation with materials would help lead them to consider unconventional options when it came to making books.

Meanwhile, all around the Workshop, the interest in artists' books was intensifying. In New York art historian Lucy Lippard was so enraptured by their potential that she wrote an essay in which she talked about these books finding their way to supermarket checkout lines. This excitement (which Lippard would rather quickly repudiate) was based on the ability of the artist's book to subvert the mainstream gallery and museum system through the creation of non-precious artifacts that could be easily duplicated and passed from hand to hand or sent through the mail. To help promote these books, Lippard and eleven partners, including the conceptual artist Sol LeWitt, founded Printed Matter bookstore in Manhattan's TriBeCa neighborhood in 1976.

The fledgling artists' book movement was hardly concentrated on women. If the intention was to subvert the gallery system, the main players were names familiar in the gallery milieu. David Hockney, Jim Dine, Dieter Roth, Ed Ruscha and Robert Motherwell were among the artists whose more than 250 works were included in the 1973 exhibition *Artists Books* at the Moore College of Art in Philadelphia, possibly the first time the term was used. But Lippard saw a specific linkage between the medium and its feminist practitioners:

> The book as a field onto which the viewer projects her own meanings
> is a potentially effective medium for a new kind of communication.
> It offers a sensibility particularly suited to a visual approach and a
> collage aesthetic, a fragmentation focusing on relationships between
> parts rather than on their stylistic peculiarities. Much more than male
> artists, women artists understand this and avoid pontification and
> aggressive pointlessness.
> Lucy Lippard. Surprises: An anthological introduction to some
> women [sic] artists' books. *Chrysalis* 5: 1977.

In the same article Lippard attempts to categorize themes in artists' books by women. Her list ranges from violence to politics to autobiography to time itself; while she never concedes the point, the range is so broad that she is unable to come up with a cohesive listing. A year later in *Chrysalis*, Judith Hoffberg, an art librarian who, as an early champion of artists' books founded her own magazine, *Umbrella*, to celebrate them, compiled a bibliography of more than 150 books by 105 women artists, from Kathy Acker to Rachel Youdelman. Hoffberg's main criterion for these books was that "they reveal an original graphic style rather than a textual emphasis."

Throughout the early 1970s as the Women's Studio Collective developed and grew, artists' books increasingly had a presence in the studio programming. At their weekly salons the participating women worked on altered books and created small edition photocopy books in a collaborative learning environment. These salons, led by Leoff Burge, were established to allow women to experience working with a woman instructor, since there were none at SUNY New Paltz, where three of the four founders had met. (Leoff Burge, several years older than the other women, had done some teaching at Dutchess Community College, where she was told that she would be hired only until they found a male replacement.)

A watershed year for the Collective came in 1976. With more than 300 artists passing through the James Street facilities that year, the founders knew that changes were necessary. First, they incorporated as a non-profit organization, with an Executive Director (Kalmbach) and an Artistic Director (Kellner). These titles were only formalities at this point; it would be another year before any of the staff received salaries. The incorporation also necessitated a name change. The State of New York didn't permit any non-profit organization to have the word collective in its title, so the Women's Studio Collective became the Women's Studio Workshop. Kalmbach would later say that the word collective was simply too pink.

Kalmbach and Kellner visited Printed Matter, where they bought books like Suzanne Lacy's *Rape Is*. This book, a subversion of the Charles Schultz phenomenon *Happiness Is* and an indictment against sexual abuse toward women, was done on the other side of the country, first at the Feminist Art Program at California Institute for the Arts and then at the Feminist Studio Workshop, part of the Los Angeles Woman's Building. The FSW took a more institutionalized path toward the development of women's creative voices by establishing a program in feminist art education that was both formal and outside the mainstream academic institutions. The Feminist Studio Workshop in the west and the Women's Studio Workshop in the east grew up together with evidently very little knowledge of each other's philosophies and daily methodologies. Both institutions, in their different ways, came to embrace artists' books as a primary medium.

Most of the artists' books in WSW's growing library were of the modest, stapled variety, as they would later describe them, printed in small but open editions, the type of artist's book that dominated the 1970s and which were coined "democratic multiples" by Museum of Modern Art librarian Clive Philpott, an ex-patriate Englishman whose strong views on the medium would come to dominate collection policies in art libraries for decades. The production method for the bulk of these books was by offset printing. By 1981, WSW had added offset to their range of production equipment; their press resided in the garage behind the James Street studios, with layout tables for pre-press production on the second floor of the main house.

Kalmbach, who was in charge of the offset shop, had learned to print at her church in Rochester, New York. The church, a large and venerable institution that had held the funerals of both Frederick Douglass and Susan B. Anthony, had an extensive print shop at which Kalmbach learned how to make hand-drawn plates, a somewhat unusual practice at that time with offset. The WSW press was purchased to print *Voices*, an edition of 500 books that documented women's work in Ulster County, one of the many projects that WSW undertook to stay connected with the local community. Through grants by the Comprehensive Employment and Training Act, a government-funded program, WSW was able to hire women to run the press; their first printer was a woman named Sky, who named the press Chutzpah, perhaps because women press operators were unusual in the 1980s. Cynthia Marsh, the offset printer from the LA Woman's Building, taught Kalmbach to develop halftones at the School of Printing at Rochester Institute of Technology. Ultimately WSW decided to discontinue offset printing because of space and technical considerations.

Even before the addition of offset facilities, Kellner, whose main work was with photo etching, had been looking for alternatives to this process, whose toxicity she found increasingly concerning. One attempt to move to a less toxic medium had her experimenting with making three-dimensional prints out of paper. After Kellner had burned out every yard sale and Goodwill store blender in the Rosendale area trying to pulp rag paper to make cast forms, WSW raised funds to hire a papermaker. Lynn Forgach came to the workshop to set up a papermaking studio and provide basic instruction to Kellner and other artists interested in the medium.

Kellner's work with photos did help lead her to explore issues of sequence in her art. In 1979, Kellner made her first artist's book, *Suspender Saga*, an accordion photo book that shows Kalmbach dressing up in various styles of men's suspenders. The book, like all of the earliest books produced at the Workshop, had no text. *Suspender Saga* became in effect the first book of WSW's artists' book program, an event that went largely unheralded, most likely because an overall program plan was not yet in place.

No books were published at WSW in 1980, but in 1981 Kellner made a series of three books that she collectively refers to as the leg books. *Nice Knees*, *Jeez Knees* and *Great Gams* all used the same black-and-white graphic photo technique as *Suspender Saga* in simply bound silkscreen books. The legs in the books are treated as straightforward linear structures as well as objects of sexuality when the photos imply their connection to a more intimate part of the body. Kellner describes the series as a way of comparing photo and drawn images by using bodily lines and curves. The fact that Kalmbach modeled for these and several other of Kellner's books is unacknowledged (Kalmbach is often recognizable, but no faces appear in the Legs series). Kellner claims that Kalmbach's enjoyment of posing was a further incentive for the early books, since she had a ready source of subject matter. The choice of her life partner and the subtle suggestions of sexuality (the three legs books) and sexual identity (*Suspender Saga*) in these early books suggest an intentional inclusion of the body issues and female sexuality that dominated so much of 1970s art. These books are light-hearted and unselfconscious; Kellner was both aware of and amused by the often overly serious handling of issues of the body and sexual identity in second-wave feminist art.

The year 1981 also saw the publication of *4x4*, a collaborative book done by the four co-founders of WSW. In a way this book marked the beginning of the artist books program at the Workshop, since all four of the women, by producing their respective four pages in the book, acknowledged the book as a vehicle for their own art. Since Wetzel had left WSW a year earlier to pursue her interests in art and music in New York City, the book also confirmed the continuing importance of all four women to the mission of WSW. None of these early books by the WSW founders was grant funded. The books were in essence demonstrations of what WSW could accomplish in their own studios on a small budget.

The following year brought the first round of jurying for the publication and artist's book residency programs, heralding a process that would eventually lead to WSW's position as the single largest publisher of handmade artists' books in the U.S. The inaugural juror was Joan Lyons. Lyons travelled from Rochester, where she directed the Visual Studies Workshop Press, to evaluate proposals from the first group of artists to apply for the new artist's book production grants. Lyons chose four projects. Two of that first cohort of books, by artists Sharon Gilbert and Susan King, went on to become iconic works from the time period.

Sharon Gilbert's *A Nuclear Atlas* is a prime example of Lippard's collage aesthetic and the genre of books from this period that dealt with the pressing issues of the potential for nuclear disaster. Printed by offset in an edition of 500 copies and perfect bound, the book combines snippets of news articles with maps and grainy photos of men in full hazmat gear. Susan King's *Women and Cars* employed a new structure designed by conservator Hedi Kyle, who initially created it as a way of organizing samples of the materials she used in her conservation practice. The structure uses an accordion spine to which are attached a series of stiff cards; by gluing some of the cards on one side of the accordion fold and some on the other, when the book is opened the cards flare out to form a pattern. The structure has come to be referred to as the flag structure, and is ubiquitous in book art workshops and exhibitions.

King was the first artist who incorporated textual content into the structure. In the book she tells the story, in anecdote and quotes from various writers, of some of the female members of her own family and finally herself and their relationship with what is usually considered the male domain of cars. King, who would eventually complete two books at WSW, is the only one of the 105 artists listed in Judith Hoffberg's 1978 roster of women artist's book publishers who later published through WSW.

Once King finished her 1983 residency she was asked back to act as juror for a new round of artists' books proposals. In keeping with their collective ideals, the WSW founders decided at the beginning of their publication grants program not to rely on their own choices. They instead decided on a rotating jury, usually including one artist who was a previous recipient of an artist's book residency grant. In this way the variety of artists' books published by WSW has remained diverse and lively. While there are obvious risks with this style (although WSW tries to avoid one type of risk by choosing the jurors after the proposals are filed, thus eliminating the possibility of a juror encouraging friends to apply during her jury year), the rotating jury does guarantee an expansive stable of artists working in a variety of media with widely varying content.

Kalmbach and Kellner used these two years to begin their collaborative book work under the name KaKeArt, an acronym made from the first two letters of their last names. Their first collaborative book, *Scene around Rosendale*, is a group of postcards that represent the type of postcards found in many small towns in rural America. Some of the images are historic images of Rosendale, the location of the Workshop as well as their home, but others are photos made by Kellner of Kalmbach in their apartment. Still others are taken from generic found postcards. *Scene Around Rosendale* became the first of several books to be referred to as *A Piece of KaKeArt*. While Kalmbach and Kellner collaborated and Kellner continued making her own books (*Me?* was completed in 1982) both Wetzel (*Sea Ribbons*) and Leoff Burge (*Kunst Comix: a phony art history*) contributed a second book to the growing collection.

The books published in the earliest years reflect not only the diversity of the artists and their content, but also a broad range of materials, structures, and production methods. Two books demonstrate the breadth of production used during this time. *Empress Bullet: an allegory* by Louise Odes Neaderland (1982) belongs to the category of books designed on a copy machine. This is the type of book that helped give rise to the term multiple. In addition to the copier (identified in the colophon as a Xerox 9400) the book, which was ultimately offset printed, makes early use of appropriated text and imagery, both taken in this case from *The New York Times*. Neaderland describes the book as being created from "… multiple copies of a single image arranged in such a way as to create a visual narrative moving through time and space with discovered poetry emerging from re-aligned text." The story, written by *Times* reporter Steve Crist (it is not clear whether it is used with his permission) is about a race horse, the eponymous Empress Bullet, a horse who found herself riderless at Aqueduct racetrack and was ultimately "destroyed" after impaling herself on a section of the rail. Both the story and the single image (by Vic DeLucia) are produced using a step-and-repeat technique engineered directly on the copier. Despite the use of the word multiple in the colophon, which would define the book as an open edition with no quantitative limitation, there is a note that the book was limited to 100 copies. Making 100 copies of many of WSW's early books assured their place on the shelves of Printed Matter, which used that minimum edition size as one parameter for the kind of work the bookstore would carry.

Headdress (1983), another early KaKeArt book is, in contrast to *Empress Bullet*, a rich and colorful evocation of form following function. Described by Kalmbach and Kellner as a wearable artist book [sic], the book is a long accordion with a folded opening at the top where the wearer can put her head. There are twelve images by Kellner of Kalmbach wearing party hats and striking silly poses. Even the title, a large Art Deco fatface type, gets in on the act. The multi-colored silkscreen production, accordion fold, and cloud-and-lightning bolt closure, and even the purely visual content are a harbinger of more complex forms to come. The book was done in an edition of seventy-five, an implicit acknowledgement that this was not the sort of production that would interest Printed Matter. The colophon says that the book was "published at WSW Print Center," terminology that was not repeated.

Once the books began to be published, WSW needed to find a market for them. Aside from Printed Matter, by now incorporated as a non-profit after realizing how poorly sales were going (so much for Lippard's supermarket checkout line sales), there were very few places in the country selling artists' books or their cousins, small press books. WSW found an early market at the American Craft Council shows and in museum libraries. Leta Stathacos at the Albright-Knox Museum in Buffalo, New York, was a particularly strong supporter of the early work.

In the 1990s the Workshop decided to cash in on the catalogue sales craze by publishing a catalogue of their handmade papers, which by this time they were producing in factory-like quantities. They added the artists' books on some extra pages at the back of the catalogue only to discover that the books were selling better than the paper (the market for which was beginning to be hurt by the influx of inexpensive papers from India and other Far Eastern manufacturers). As they concentrated on marketing the books, they met booksellers like the late Tony Zwicker, whose generosity to them was mirrored in her dealings with nearly every artist bookmaker with whom she worked. It was Zwicker who guided WSW toward university libraries. On a trip back from Florida where they travelled to close up the home of Kellner's parents after the death of Kellner's father, Kalmbach and Kellner made sales calls at universities along the way. Special Collections in academic libraries would eventually become by far the largest purchasers of WSW books.

The fourteen books published in 1982 and 1983 helped to set the pace at which the artists' books would be selected, funded, and produced; ultimately WSW would settle on publishing seven books a year. (For some years men were invited to apply, but once grants for artists to work in their home studios were halted, WSW decided to only accept women for the residency grants. Six books by men are in the collection.) The guidelines suggest that the artists consider editions of between fifty and 100 books, although as the books have grown more complex the editions have, not surprisingly, shrunk somewhat to a current number that generally ranges from twenty-five to fifty. Thematically there are patterns: Family, relationships, and domestic life, particularly centered around food, tend to dominate the list; many of these use memory as the primary narrative device. The book as a political act has had a strong presence at WSW since *A Nuclear Atlas*. Kalmbach and

Kellner's enduring interest in political discourse has helped to feed this category; they have contributed half a dozen books either singly or under the KaKeArt imprint with overt political content. Several of the books have a strongly conceptual basis; some of these also focus on science and nature. There have been surprisingly few books over the years that have specifically focused on issues of women and the body, although the subject is implicit in a number of the books.

To Kellner, editioning is at the basis of artists' books; whatever they are, unique objects are not artists' books in her definition. Kalmbach's concerns rest more with the increasing focus on form over content, a trend she sees as potentially damaging to the integrity of the books. In the meantime, the vision of Kalmbach and Kellner, so prescient in 1979, and their continuing rich collaboration, remain the driving forces behind Women's Studio Workshop's artists' book program.

On a recent morning in the Workshop's bright front room, studio manager Chris Petrone works closely with a ceramic artist who is exploring printmaking as a medium. In her even voice, Petrone explains techniques new to the artist, working with her to wipe the plates, mix inks, and crank the etching press. As Kellner passes through the studio, she, too, stops to describe a technique; the next day Kellner herself will spend the morning working with the same artist. In this manner Women's Studio Workshop continues to feed the artists fortunate to pass through its doors. WSW is no longer a collective, but the spirit of sharing and encouragement that has driven the Workshop for more than thirty-five years has not changed, a testament to the four art desperados who continue so many years later to guide and shape its mission. As in 1974, the main work of Women's Studio Workshop is, in the end, women making art.

A PRESENCE OF THE PAST:

MY WORK AS A STORYTELLER IN

THE ARTISTS' BOOK MEDIUM

CLARISSA SLIGH

Memory and the act of remembering play a major role in my artwork. I speak from the intersection of many narratives: my life, family, community, and nation as well as that of a human being on our planet. Within each frame of reference, I am both insider and outsider. Much like a book, I am the form and its contents. Each fragment of a memory or a dream is an opportunity to open a door, to explore, to deconstruct, to re-combine, to transform, and to inspire. Where it takes me is not always comfortable, but if I can hang out with the memory and the experience that the memory brings, the story that I have to tell will come. It is like listening to a single instrument and gradually becoming aware of the other instruments in the orchestra.

For long stretches of time, I gave up on my dream of making art. When I decided to reclaim that part of my life in the 1980s, I knew I had to find a way to work from the inside out. There was much I did not want to reveal about my life. How could I express the unspeakable, the unseeable? At that time, I was living in New York City, where many artists knew how to articulate their vision. I had come from a small black community in Virginia. My reality seemed different. How could I show visually something of the way that the Baptist preacher and the gospel and rhythm-and-blues singers and musicians of my youth used repetitive, rhythmic fragments to elicit the audience response necessary for the satisfactory completion of their work? How could I create a space in which the viewers could respond openly to my work with their own feelings and emotions, an intimate space that could be held close or pushed away at the viewer's leisure?

To begin making visual images again, I gave myself an assignment to make one self-portrait a day for a year. The daily drawing was to express my experience of that day as well as to create discipline in this endeavor. At that time I was working on Wall Street and it was a huge challenge to shift from the mindset of numbers to the task of drawing. But I felt like I would wither and die if I did not learn to express my interior ideas in a visual form.

At the end of nine months, when some artists saw the images and immediately understood what I had done, I was surprised. Those rough and crude drawings had been done for my eyes only. All the things that had happened in my life seemed invisible. It was the enthusiastic response of those artists that enabled me to deepen my search for my own voice. I asked myself, "What do you know about?" "Who are you?" Buried within me was an accumulation of all the unanswered questions I had ever asked.

I began my new work with family snapshots and fragments of stories I remembered about my life before I left home. It took shape as a series of constructed photographic images and texts. Sometimes the pictures suggested the words. Sometimes the words came first. Eventually I had no pictures, only words. That's when I turned to the book form.

Today when I begin a project there is usually an idea in mind, but the real narrative unfolds in the process of putting it together. An inner voice takes over and asks, "And then what happened?" or "That's not what happened!" or "What makes you think that?" Some answers come from within; some come from other sources as a new story begins to take shape.

Historical research is often an important part of my process. I love uncovering fragments of stories from other times. I use them to reconstruct and question history as it comes to me rather than perpetuate what I have always been told. I believe that the artist is a shaman, a spiritual medium, a way show-er and a poet, who draws on intuition, personal experiences, and things inherited from ancestral communal memories. How could it be otherwise? My narratives may be partially fabricated in the telling, but it is truth I speak. When I was growing up truth was found in books. But I knew my story was missing.

In 2004 when I decided to make an artist's book to commemorate the 50th anniversary of the Supreme Court's 1954 *Brown vs. Board of Education* decision, I drew on my memory of my mother's determination to have her children go to the best public schools where we lived. Designated "for whites only," I remember riding my school bus past those well-built structures. When she enrolled my siblings and me in the local school desegregation court case, my mother could not have imagined the many social changes that would take place in Arlington from 1954 to 2004.

I wanted the narratives for *It Wasn't Little Rock* to show the evolution of an aspect of that change. Since my mother was no longer alive in 2004, I pieced together the stories she had told me about her life while I was growing up. From an earlier installation called the Witness Project, I had videotapes of my sisters and brother and my daughter telling their stories about how they experienced the desegregated schools. It was like bringing out the family album. Each person told the story of each picture differently. Their voices, added to my interpretation of the events, and interwoven with excerpts from news clippings and legal documents, gave the narrative much more complexity and depth.

Another group of narratives, *Wrongly Bodied* and *Wrongly Bodied Two*, came out of my documentary project of photographing Deb transitioning to Jake. In the beginning, I thought of the project as gathering evidence in the form of photographs.

However, nothing could have prepared me for the complexity or intensity of the act. Even after reading the literature that was available in the mid-1990s, it was difficult for me to wrap my head around gender dysphoria. Jake, however, really wanted me to understand how he came to his decision to undergo numerous surgical and chemical changes to his body. I videotaped our conversations.

Why tell Jake's story? Since I am not transgender, can I be trusted to do that? In order to understand a desire for a change of identity of this magnitude, I associated Jake's desire with another change of identity that comes out of the black community. The history of light skin blacks "passing" for whites in this country and all the related debates around transgression and authenticity helped me to understand Jake's anxiety and the importance of his story. While I was a witness to Jake's transition process, *Wrongly Bodied* is not simply Jake's story. It is also my story. When you are close to a person as they question their identity, you have to question your identity, too. I began to think about the fact that I would never be able to change my brown skin and "pass" for anything other than what I have been—a black woman.

This has presented many opportunities for a very rich life. Living in New York City often felt lonely and isolating. It was from that place that I organized and co-hosted a gathering: *It Is Time To End Our Isolation: Women of African Descent in the Visual Arts*. Out of that exciting and electrifying experience came the idea to create *Coast to Coast: A Women of Color National Artist's Book Project*. It was for that project, in 1987, that I completed my first artist's book, *What's Happening With Momma?* During a Women's Studio Workshop residency the next year, Ann Kalmbach guided me in creating a silk-screen and letterpress edition of the book. The year after that, I created *Reading Dick and Jane With Me*. Despite having made these two books, I didn't think of myself as an artist bookmaker. Photographically based prints and text-based installations had formed the core of my work. As part of my process, I work in a much larger format and explore a combination and permutation of ideas before translating a story into the book medium. But with artists' books I can combine my love of books and my desire to tell stories that are still missing from mainstream books.

My world of today is very different from the world of my parents or the world of my childhood or even the world of much of my adulthood. Ultimately, my work comes out of a strong desire to embrace who and what I am in this place and time and to commemorate and celebrate the presence of the past.

CLARISSA SLIGH IS AN ARTIST, LECTURER, AND WRITER WHO WEAVES TOGETHER THE PERSONAL, POLITICAL, AND HISTORICAL IN PHOTOGRAPHS, PRINTS, ARTISTS' BOOKS, AND TEXT-BASED INSTALLATIONS.

BOOKS AS BRIDGES

EMILY SPEED In Flatland, by Edwin A. Abbott, the narrator goes to Spaceland, a world he first sees from above, which appears to be two-dimensional, made up of flat lines on a page. He changes position and realizes that when viewed from another angle, this world actually has a third dimension. On returning to his home in Flatland, he tries to explain this revelation, but is thought mad because no one there can conceive of an extra dimension. This part of the story relates to the way artists' books work for me. An artist's book may afford its viewer another kind of dimension, an imaginative realm or an insight into the artist's thought process, but it really needs to be experienced first-hand to be fully understood.

What I love about artists' books, and try to utilize, is their slipperiness. Hard to define and neither one thing nor the other, I find them an indeterminate art form and enjoy the ambiguity they offer. Slightly on the margins, I would describe artists' books as liminal spaces or thresholds. Architectonic descriptions come to mind: bridges, corridors, doorways, corners, all of these in-between spaces that link other things together.

I work in many forms: sculpture, drawing, animation, installation, performance, and artists' books. In practical terms, the books that I create are as much part of my practice as all the other things, but they perform a special kind of role, a joining one. To try and define their role further, I would liken them to bridges. When, for example, I make a book to accompany an installation, my intention is that the book might provide a bridge between the work and my thoughts, without being too literal or explicit. The book and bridge analogy also came up recently in correspondence with U.K. book artist Lucy May Schofield, who describes beautifully that artists' books "create little bridges for people, from their lives into the artists' world." My book forms also provide a place for me to combine words, materials, and imagery. In doing this, books often seem to know their own form immediately; their folds, shape, construction, and material are clear because of what I wish them to communicate.

Some of my bookworks also exist entirely apart from other work, and *Unfolding Architecture* is one of those. This book was one of the first that I ever made and completing the edition seemed like alchemy, except that I had made an idea solid. *Unfolding Architecture* is experienced through Gordon, and the story tells of how he witnesses the city he lives in unfolding, just like paper. The unfolding of the buildings leaves the city, or the site where the city once stood, an empty plain (plane) and the story ends with Gordon rolling a newspaper and seeing a glimpse of a future: the shape of a tower he will build. The book is an allegory; the architecture as metaphor for the experience of my father's dementia. There is a detached feeling about the tale as it is told by an unknown observer, all in third person and with little emotion. This plain-spoken approach fed into the appearance of the book, with firm letter-pressed text in a muted grey-purple version of black. There is also the barest hint of images present in blue-grey screen-printed line drawings. The book is not fancy or decorated because nothing about the experience was—it's a hazy period of my life where the impossible was happening and only became real in hindsight.

The accordion book is housed in a handmade balsa wood box, the sides of which fall down when the lid is lifted off, mirroring the city in the story. Giving the text this precarious and inconstant container was important, and to make something symbiotic for the content, it had to be a sculptural bookwork that folded, making the physical format echo the narrative within.

I had initial ideas about how *Unfolding Architecture* would be handled: the box as upright building; the building being laid flat; the exterior coming apart; and the interior pages being stretched out flat. Of course, how people actually handle the book is completely out of my control, but watching people look through a copy is very curious.

There is a kind of reverence for handmade books with a visible price tag. This seems to then be replaced by anxiety as the handler picks up the box and feels the insubstantial weight of this thing which, on first sight, seemed to be made of wood. They feel the vulnerability of the structure and change their grip, often setting it back down. The lid is taken off and in that moment where the walls of the box fall down, the handler panics, thinking that they have broken it. Once they realize that it is meant that way, there is relief and the inner book is picked up, gently. The handler keeps lifting it and the pages keep opening out flat until it comes out of the box. Second horror! Is it meant to do that? Yes, they realize, it is, and then they start to read the words. As the book is put back in the box, the drawing of the tower on drafting paper, sitting at the bottom, is seen and hopefully makes sense there, being the next chapter of the story and also the end.

There is something special about the fact that books have their own past and are so rooted in history, yet they exist happily in contemporary works. This history means that books make immediate sense to people; they are familiar, known entities. Although artists' books may contain the unexpected (collapsing walls for example), people already know what to do with them. In some ways then, they can be an introduction to my work, or a way to communicate difficult concepts in a trustworthy object.

The haptic nature of artists' books appeals to me and that exploration or journey that the viewer takes while looking through a book makes it quite distinct from other art forms. I want to make things that can be touched and that provide a personal, intimate experience for the viewer. Artists' books are marvellously accessible in the respect of them being handled, especially when coupled with the fact that they are often very affordable. As bookworks are sometimes the only way I can afford to buy other artists' work, I am extremely glad I can make things that will be owned, re-experienced, and carried around.

The contradictory qualities of books captivate me: their strength and fragility; the fact that they can be both unique and handmade but also multiplied; the way they simultaneously reveal and conceal. Perhaps this production line way of making things (although I am far from machine-like!) is a respite of sorts, a concentrated, calm space to work through ideas without the guilt of inactivity.

EMILY SPEED IS AN ARTIST WORKING IN DRAWING, SCULPTURE, PERFORMANCE, INSTALLATION, AND ARTISTS' BOOKS. SHE WORKS IN LIVERPOOL, U.K.

There is great satisfaction to be had from putting all the elements together and considering the layers of meaning. There is also the pleasure of producing editions and the physical processes involved. The repetition of printing and binding means that by the end of production I know the work incredibly well. The endless qualities of what an artist's book can be provide much to engage with, explore, and subvert. Put simply, I like making books.

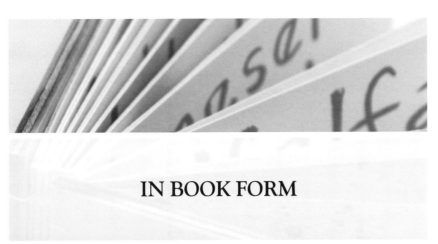

IN BOOK FORM

I studied art with Abstract Expressionist painters at The New School of Art in **SUSAN MILLS** Toronto. The first year we worked exclusively in black and white. The first semester we drew in black and white every day from 9 a.m. until 5 p.m. The second semester we painted in black and white every day from 9 until 5. Art was a daily sequence. I still have teacher Robert Markle's long list of required reading for artists, including Walker Evans' and James Agee's *Let Us Now Praise Famous Men*, Georges Seurat's *The Drawings*, and Eadweard Muybridge's motion studies.

I studied conceptual art at Nova Scotia College of Art and Design in Halifax, Nova Scotia. I was in the Intermedia program – video, performance, and books. This area included time-based work that used the small screen, the body, and the page as alternate spaces for art practice. I worked in book form and thought of my work as video for a shy person. I have worked in book form exclusively ever since and the definition of artists' books as time-based and using the page as an alternate space is still resonant for me. Books that were important to me as a student include Ed Ruscha's *Twentysix Gasoline Stations*, and André Breton's *Nadja*. I found these books in the library when I was assigned to write an essay on Robert Frank's *The Americans*. I liked *Twentysix Gasoline Stations* for looking so clean and tablet-like and *Nadja* for the illustrations and the very cool cover of the 1960 Grove Press edition. The essay I wrote on *The Americans* was a multi-level critique of contemporary late capitalism, parroting the lectures of Benjamin Buchloh, Martha Rosler, and Allan Sekula. I wrote without ever looking at the book, in the same way that I might have written about a painting I had never seen. In this case, unrecognized by me, Robert Frank was my hard-working and astute rural Nova Scotia neighbor, who I liked very much, and whose work in my own experience had no link to capitalism. I knew his poetic Polaroids and collages that were published as *The Lines of My Hand*. In conjunction, I studied feminism and art with Mary Kelly when she was exhibiting installations of her *Post-Partum Document* in London. In her class, we re-examined Freud's *The Interpretation of Dreams* and the mirror stage of Jacques Lacan. She encouraged us to read the original sources. I worked on a semester-long, text-based bookwork, moving from "who is she" to "we take our father's names". The unbound, pocket pages of hardware store plastic and duct tape contained pages from my diary and real objects like a diaphragm. At the end of the term I felt too naked to exhibit this work. *Diary* was a student work that imitated *Post-Partum Document*, but the location was my own.

For several years after art school I house-sat for writer and screenwriter Rudy Wurlitzer. His house had amazing books. *The Collected Works of Billy the Kid* by Michael Ondaatje, the drawn storyboard book for a never-produced movie of *Dune*, and a broadside about Nikola Tesla are three that I remember.

I continued to make artists' books.

With a Canada Council art grant I moved to New York City. I wanted to learn more about books, to be able to bind my books, and to order the sequence.

I wanted my book works to look like regular books.

I apprenticed as a bookbinder with bookbinder/artist Richard Minsky in New York.

I studied bookbinding privately with bookbinder/artist Daniel Kelm in Northampton, Massachusetts.

I took many bookbinding workshops.

I taught a bookbinding class at NSCAD.

I taught an evening bookbinding class at Cooper Union Continuing Education.

I worked as a hand bookbinder.

I continued to work in book form.

I made phase boxes for two years at Franklin Furnace, an artists' books archive. I boxed (and read) the Fluxus books. My favorites were from Dick Higgins' Something Else Press.

I was invited to substitute-teach a binding class at Women's Studio Workshop in Rosendale, New York. Imposition programs were forthcoming for home computers. Dick Higgins and Alison Knowles were in that class, preparing for the release of this new program.

I took a weekend workshop at WSW with Barbara Bash. We worked exclusively in black and white. We made big brushes of unusual materials and also wrote/performed/danced with her person-sized horsehair brush dipped in a bucket of ink. Afterwards, I started to work simultaneously very large and very small and to think about text as performance.

WSW published *Ruderal Plants in Manhattan*, my first and only large edition (100) book, and my first and only artist residency. I was and am very happy to be part of the WSW book collection. This book seemed to cross a line from an artist's book to literary book. I was described as "collaborating with myself".

Interested in poetry, I started taking writing workshops at St. Mark's Poetry Project in New York. Slowly, text disappeared from the surface of my book pages. I "wrote" about what was not said. Words were implied. Language was internal.

I noticed that more and more artists' books, often utilizing letterpress, were collaborations between poets and artists. The books were literary and collected by libraries rather than galleries. Poets seemed amazed that their books sold for so much money while artists seemed amazed that their work in book form sold for so little.

I continue making books without words.

My bookbinding class at NSCAD was renamed Book Arts.

I study Butoh at Cave in Brooklyn. I performed a piece, *Butoh Flip Book*, where I am mostly naked, painted white, and upside down. This was not a book for a shy person.

I continue to make books in a tiny studio in Nova Scotia and a tiny studio in Manhattan.

I continue to work as a binder-for-hire and to teach bookbinding.

Last year I founded Full Tilt, a very tiny artists' books school.

I continue to work without words.

SUSAN MILLS IS AN ARTIST WHO WORKS IN BOOK FORM. SHE LIVES AND WORKS IN NEW YORK CITY AND IN CAPE BRETON, NOVA SCOTIA.

MAKING IT RIGHT:

INTERVIEW WITH ERICA VAN HORN

KATHLEEN WALKUP In 1974 Erica Van Horn was a young artist on a mission. Having left her native New Hampshire after one year of college to head west like many young people in the 1970s, Van Horn wanted to study art. What she found in the San Francisco Bay Area was a rich center of art practice, along with some expensive places to study it. She also discovered a legendary printmaker named Misch Kohn; even better, he was teaching in the bargain-priced state system. Van Horn enrolled at California State University Hayward (now CSU East Bay). Kohn proved a wise mentor, and at the end of her studies at Hayward he recommended that she do her graduate work away from the Bay Area, at the School of the Art Institute of Chicago.

For Van Horn, these moves back and forth across the US proved a harbinger of her future. Van Horn has lived and worked in New York, Paris, Italy, London, and the English countryside. In each place it has been the quotidian, what she calls the small details, that have informed her work. She is an observer and a recorder, someone always slightly at the edge of the activity whose focus remains on the aspects of life that those settled in it might miss from being too close.

In 1988 Van Horn was introduced to the English poet and publisher Simon Cutts, the principal in Coracle Press. Cutts and Van Horn established a work and life partnership that has combined her love of living in new places (portability) with his desire to continue publishing (books to be stored), while both continue to make art. Today they are living in still another location, the green hills of Tipperary, Ireland.

KW: SO WHEN DID YOU BEGIN MAKING BOOKS?

Well, officially my first book was made on the day President Kennedy was shot. I went home and started recording everything and later my mother showed me how to sew that together.

But I really got going with books when I went to the School of the Art Institute in Chicago, where I took a course in bookbinding. I loved it, I loved making these objects, but very quickly I got tired of blank books. And so I started incorporating my prints first into the covers and then the end papers. And I was just doing more and more to make the book something that was mine rather than just another blank book. But I didn't actually incorporate it into my own work until a few years later when I was traveling and I didn't have a studio. That's when I started using the book as a very portable art form.

KW: HOW DID YOU END UP TRAVELING IN EUROPE?

I got an NEA grant, which was just so wonderful, I was given money and I could do what I wanted with it. I had applied in the category of books; I had done a few things, more like boxes, clamshell boxes with conglomerations of things in them. And I was calling those books.

I was in the process of ending a relationship; I thought I might as well just go to Europe. I was so interested in medieval art and medieval imagery. I wanted to go see it. My plan, being a good New Englander, was to make the money last as long as I could. I went to France and started looking at books and paintings. And then I would start drawing, and making books. Mostly they were long hand painted accordion books. I wouldn't say they were faux-medieval, but I was trying very hard to draw and to make pattern in that way that had been done.

KW: IN TERMS OF WHAT MIGHT HAVE SPARKED YOUR IMAGINATION OR CREATIVITY WITH BOOKS, DO YOU HAVE ANY SENSE ABOUT WORK THAT YOU LOOKED AT, SOMEBODY ELSE'S WORK THAT YOU SAW, THINGS THAT MIGHT HAVE RESONATED WITH YOU, THAT MADE YOU THEN THINK ABOUT THE BOOK AS A MEDIUM?

It was all historical. I wasn't aware of the world of books being made. And when I did see things it was always those illustrated books, a heavy letterpress poem and then someone illustrating it. It was a book as a beautiful object.

For me, someone like Ed Ruscha was so far from what I was interested in, that it was not relevant. I had been slightly put down in graduate school. Every time I used sewing in my work, that was girl art, and that was a definite negative thing.

I think I've been a kind of lonely artist. I was never part of a group sensibility. And in some ways I think that helped me to blaze my own trail. Sometimes when I would see what other artists had done, I'd be very excited. When I started working with Tony Zwicker, a whole world of books opened up to me. There was so much I didn't know about what other people were doing.

KW: SO YOUR TIME IN EUROPE MUST HAVE FED THAT ISOLATION.

Once I left Chicago, and I went to Paris, I was separated by language, and I was separated by nationality. I was not the right kind of woman in France, I was just not. I was a mess, in my thrift store clothes. And so my isolation was more, I was very busy trying to survive on very little, to make my money last, and to spend as much time in the museums. So again I didn't become part of things, I didn't pay attention. And I really did start making books because it was what I could do. If I were staying in a hotel or I lived on a boat for awhile, I didn't have a lot of space. It was always about working in small spaces and I had little film canisters with my paints mixed up and things like that. I even had this nightgown that I used to wear when I was painting. It didn't matter if it was all painty, because nobody was seeing it. I wasn't involved in the art world; I was just making things.

KW: DID YOU THINK OF YOURSELF AN ARTIST?

Yes, but I didn't think any further than that. In Paris I met Madeleine DesChamps, French woman who was running the American Center. She introduced me to an American artist, Kate Van Houten, who also later did a book at the Women's Studio Workshop. And through Kate I suddenly found out that there was a lot of book activity going on in Paris and I started paying attention, and I had books in some shows.

KW: YOU MENTIONED THE FACT THAT YOU MOVED TO A PLACE WITH A DIFFERENT LANGUAGE AND YOU'RE TALKING ABOUT YOUR BACKGROUND VERY MUCH AS A MAKER AND SOMEBODY WHO'S INVOLVED VISUALLY WITH ART. SO WHERE DID YOUR INTEREST IN USING LANGUAGE AS OPPOSED TO LEARNING DIFFERENT LANGUAGES COME FROM?

Perhaps some of that came from my mother who is fascinated with language and is quite eloquent. Everywhere you go you end up with different language issues. Just growing up in New Hampshire where a carbonated drink was called tonic and then out west it was soda and in the Midwest pop. I was always interested in those differences. There aren't so many in America.

KW: IF, AS YOU SAY, LANGUAGE BOTH DESCRIBES AND CREATES COMMUNITY, WHAT DOES THAT MEAN FOR YOUR WORK?

I think that I'm kind of an observer; I'm always a little bit outside wherever I am. So I work to see that community, to recognize it, to be part of it as much as I can be. And I think language is the first entry into that. But I don't really want to be trapped by a community, either; I like my outside status. I do like being an outsider, an expatriate, whatever. It's not exactly about being an expatriate; it is being outside.

KW: YOU HAVE BEEN LIVING IN EUROPE FOR MOST OF YOUR ADULT LIFE, BUT ALSO EXPRESSING YOURSELF AS STANDING OUTSIDE; YOU'RE NOT ASSIMILATING. HOW IS THAT REFLECTED IN YOUR WORK?

Here in Ireland I have this small series called "Living Locally" which followed one I did in Italy, which was called *Italian Lessons*. One of the Italian lessons was a postcard that said, "In Italy one is only allowed eleven words per postcard." If you have more than eleven words written on your postcard you have to pay a higher rate in the postage. It's like, who thought of this? It's those details that are so interesting I have to show them to other people.

I'd be arrogant to say that I'm documenting the place I'm in, but I'm documenting my attention, where my little attention goes. One of the books I did as part of the Living Locally series was called *Gifts from the Government*. It's all these odd things that you get here, like every Christmas if you buy a book of stamps you get one extra stamp and that's like your little present from the government. Just sort of small things, and I just love it, I've never lived in a place where you just sort of get these little presents. I think sometimes people can look at what I'm doing and go 'yeah, so what?' They are small things. There's nothing very profound happening. But it is the details I'm interested in. I'm interested in the things I might forget. I think that's all I do with my work.

Interview continued on page 83

Interview continued on page 83

HAND

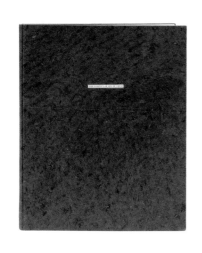

The Complex of all of These, 2009
ABIGAIL UHTEG
14" x 11" Edition 35

...nting bit by bit like so many pieces of glitter in a snow globe, cities drowning and burie... The map unfolding, the world expanding too fast for its edges, the narrator barely esc... ...ed. And so began the interminable nights despite anyone's best effort at daylight savings t... ...ng pills, warm milk), and to be fair it must be said that they began well, low voices at two in... ...ing, gentle whispers between parentheses, impervious to their inadequacy. To be fair it must be s... ...they mean well, grand overtures that spanned rivers and mountains and time zones, a discerna... ...found in the company of another, deliberate, particular. This awkward world of missed gestures a... ...understood words that claims to be the only possible reality. Cleverly concealed weakness... ...ved one April day to the clover that held the impression of their combined weights— ...erable distance (remember the persistent mountains, rivers, time zones, now rendered mu... ...and not meaning the green thing negotiated into the discernable configurations of her body and h... ...meant to walk but they'd been lost in translation and amidst miles of tangled teleph...

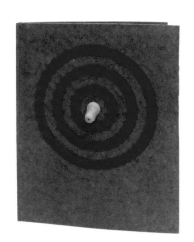

Skim Milk and Soft Wax, 2008
DANI LEVENTHAL
12.5" x 9.75" Edition 36

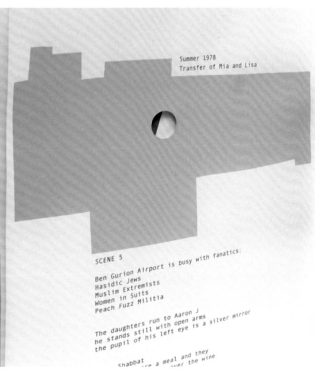

Summer 1978
Transfer of Mia and Lisa

SCENE 5

Ben Gurion Airport is busy with fanatics:
Hasidic Jews
Muslim Extremists
Women in Suits
Peach Fuzz Militia

The daughters run to Aaron J
he stands still with open arms
the pupil of his left eye is a silver mirror

Shabbat

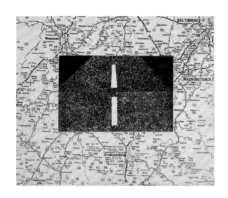

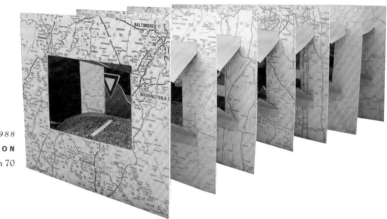

Everyday Road Signs, 1988
CAROL BARTON
7.5" x 8.75" Edition 70

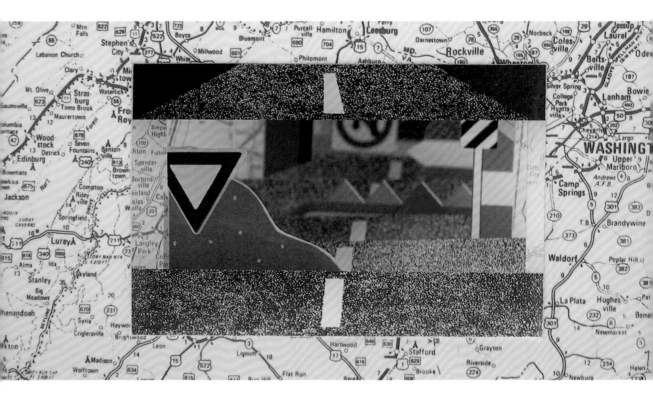

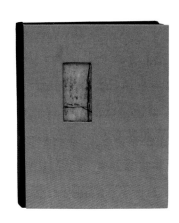

First Visit, 2001
SARA LANGWORTHY
8.75" x 7.25" Edition 40

HEADDRESS

Headdress, 1983
ANN KALMBACH AND TATANA KELLNER
5.75" x 11.75" Edition 75

Handbook of Practical
Geographies, 2004
HEATHER O'HARA
11" x 17" Edition 100

How to Eat Your Enemy, 2006
CLAIRE RAU
9" x 9" Edition 25

How I Lost My Vegetarianism

by Katherine Aoki

I was at a bar in St. Louis with a bunch of guys.
They ordered buffalo wings without asking me.
I was bored and ate one without thinking twice.

How I Lost My Vegetarianism, 1998
KATHERINE AOKI
8" x 9.75" Edition 75

the vegetables
re smothered
Velveeta...

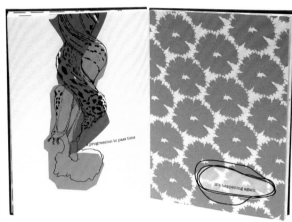

Patterned Pleasures, 2009
AMANDA KALINOSKI
7.5" x 5.25" Edition 50

they creak, hiss, and whine

Relation, 1999
ANN LOVETT
6.5" x 3.75" Edition 200

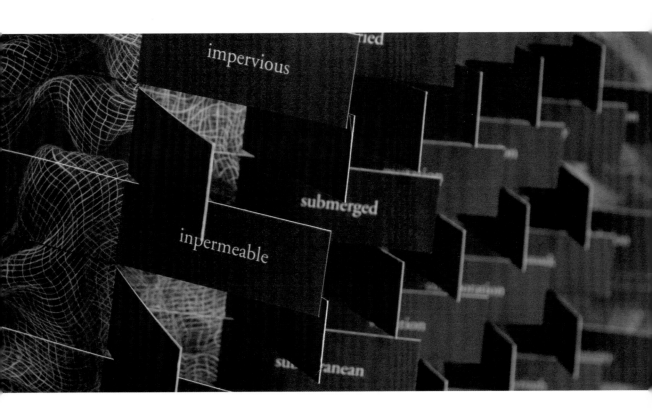

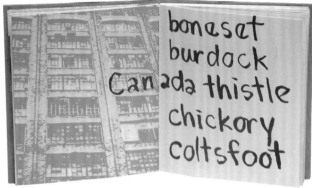

Ruderal Plants in Manhattan, 1995
SUSAN MILLS
5" x 4.75" Edition 100

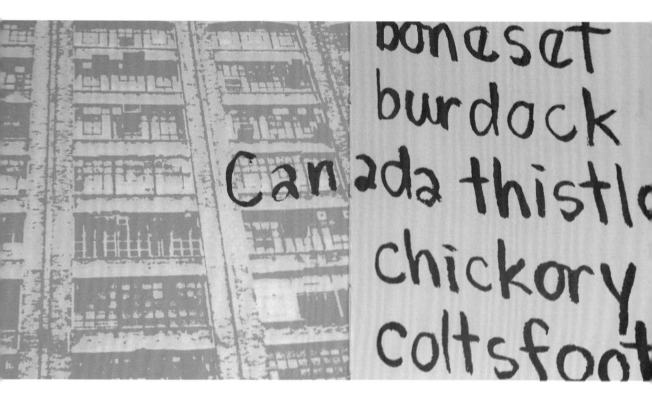

Eight Breakfasts in 8 Pages, 1999
DEBORAH FREDERICK
7.25" x 9.75" Edition 100

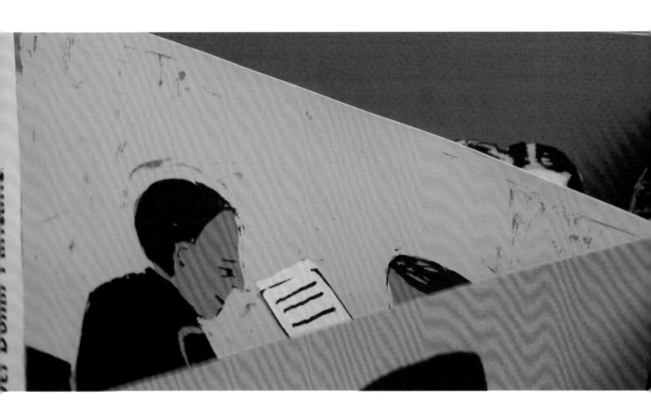

Treasure, 2008
KATIE BALDWIN
8" x 8" Edition 35

Now looking back, she
could not figure out
the actual moment when she did
start over.

※はじけない粒が少量残ります。

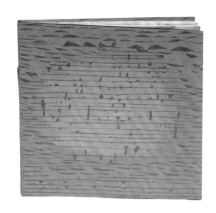

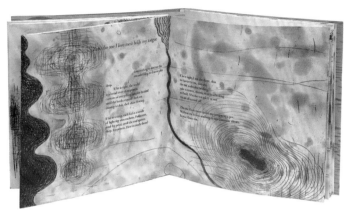

Truly Bone, 1998
KAREN KUNC
8" x 7.5" Edition 50

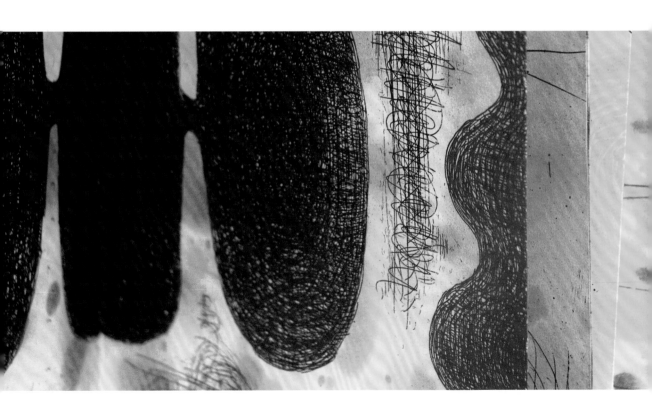

VOICE

1992 Guilin, China
Mom and dad on a tour

1971 Florida?

I said. We watched the
He put

Taichung, Taiwan

Sister saw grandma
playing a relay race,
Grandma had quite
a social life in Taiwan,
though I only knew her
as quiet
and withdrawn
in the United States.

2002 Seattle, USA

my parents but me,
dolls dad brought back
took a self-portrait
with wooden clogs

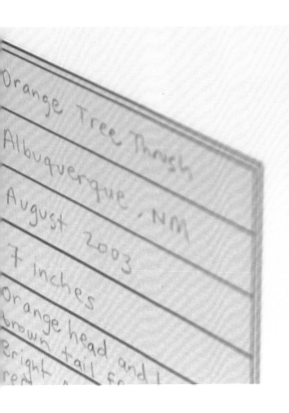

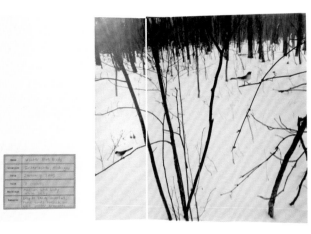

Bird Watching, 2006
PAULA MCCARTNEY
10" x 8" Edition 40

Crazy Quilt, 1998
MAUREEN CUMMINGS
10" x 10" Edition 100

0100010001001111101
001110

of the DON.

010101000100000101
010101010101000100
111101001100010011111
0100011101011001

After all his TAUTOLOGY

Errors of the Amanuensis, 2010
ANN KALMBACH AND TATANA KELLNER
8.5" x 10.75" Edition 30

0100000101001100
001100010011110100
001101010101010101
000100100101001111
01001110

Forgotten Knowledge, 2002
MARISÓL LIMON MARTINEZ
7.75" x 11.125" Edition 50

Lucha por la Vida, 2000
RAL VERONI
6" x 8.5" Edition 40

Don't Bug the Waitress, 1987
SUSAN BAKER
11.5" x 7" Edition 200

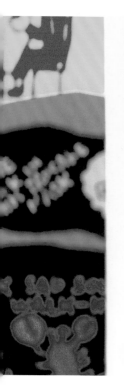

Transatlantic Balderdash, 2010
ANN KALMBACH AND TATANA KELLNER
6.75" x 12" Edition 25

Momotaro/Peach Boy, 2003

TOMIE ARAI

15.5" x 11.5" Edition 25

Pistol/Pistil: Botanical Ballistics, 1997
ANN KALMBACH AND TATANA KELLNER
8.75" x 6.75" Edition 100

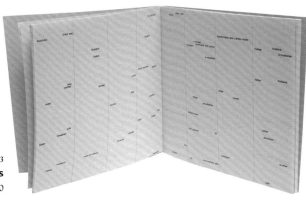

Remembrance, 2003
JUDITH MOHNS
6.5" x 6.5" Edition 400

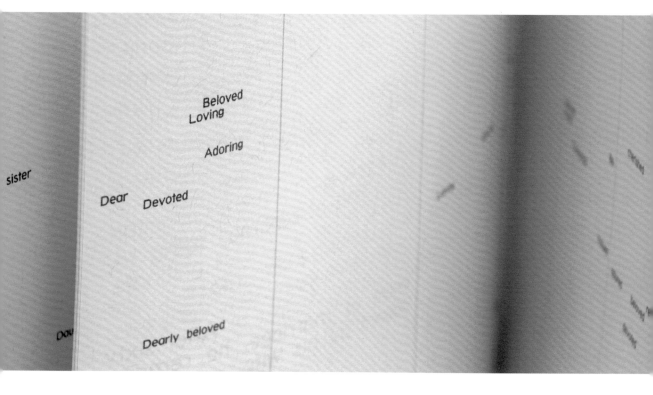

None of Your Damn Business, 2010
BARBARA LEOFF BURGE
9.125" x 7.75" Edition 50

Scattered Memory, 2005
EDIE TSONG
12" x 6.25" Edition 50

Unfolding Architecture, 2007

EMILY SPEED

8" x 3.5" Edition 90

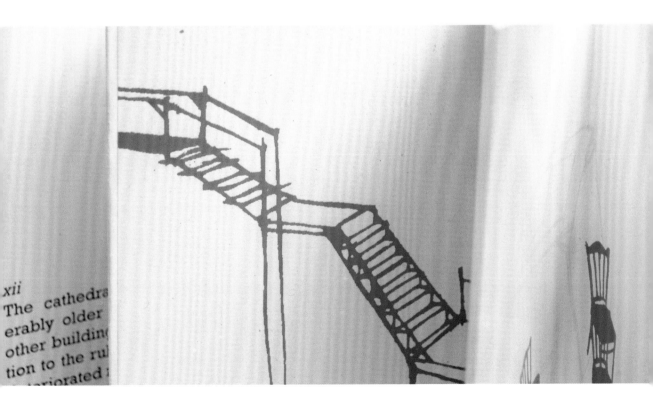

xii
The cathedra
erably older
other building
tion to the ru
eriorated

*What's Happening
with Momma?*, 1988
CLARISSA SLIGH
11.5" x 6.25" Edition 150

Women and Cars, 1983
SUSAN ELIZABETH KING
8.125" x 5.75" Edition 500

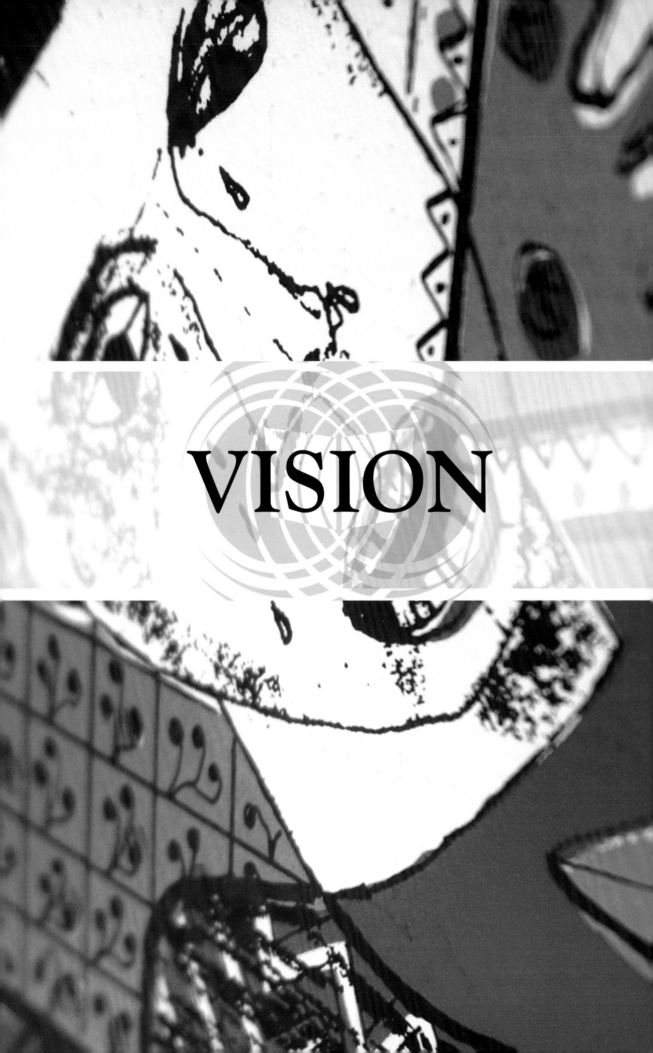

VISION

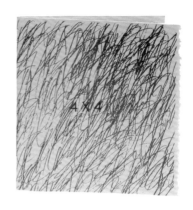

4x4, 1981

**BARBARA LEOFF BURGE, ANN KALMBACH,
TATANA KELLNER, AND ANITA WETZEL**
7.5" x 6.75" Edition 100

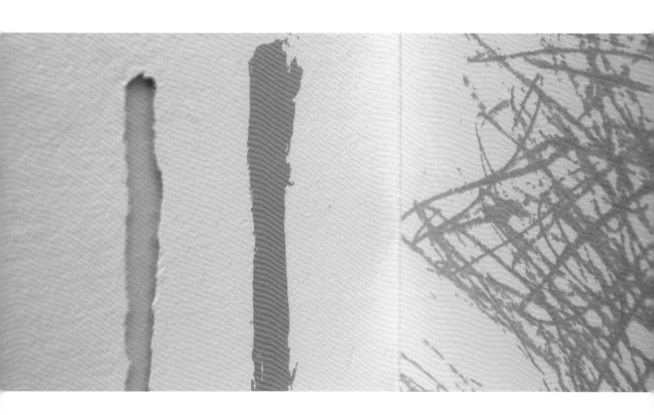

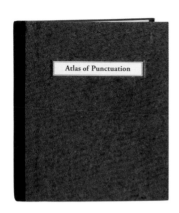

Atlas of Punctuation, 2004
HEIDI NEILSON
9.75" x 8.5" Edition 100

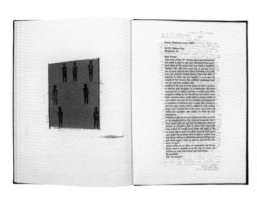

The Business is Suffering, 2003
MAUREEN CUMMINGS
13" x 9.5" Edition 50

not sold a single negro since I left Richmond. I have got the cash in Farmers Bank to hold up my draft a day or two hopeing I may yet hold enough to pay. also to pay you the $258. This is to inform you that if it comes back not pd, I shall pay it as soon as I sell I shall go to Wilmington the next week if they are not sold I shall remove them down in Chowan Co, N.C.
Say to Old Man Bill I hope he nor you will abuse me very bad, I tell I have done my best.
Yours in haste
JJ Williams

Empress Bullet, 1982
LOUISE ODES NEADERLAND
8.5" x 9.5" Edition 100

What Day Is It: An Artist's Book, 1986
KATE VAN HOUTEN
9.75" x 11.25" Edition 63

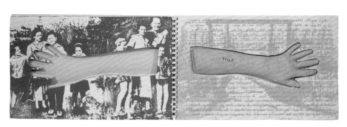

71125 *Fifty Years of Silence:*
Eva Kellner's Story, 1992
TATANA KELLNER
12" x 20" Edition 40

B-11226 Fifty Years of Silence:
Eugene Kellner's Story, 1992
TATANA KELLNER
12" x 20" Edition 50

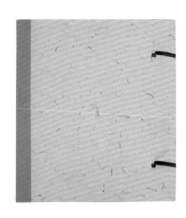

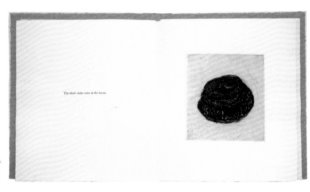

The House With Four Walls, 1991
ZARINA
16.5" x 29.5" Edition 25

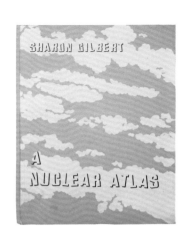

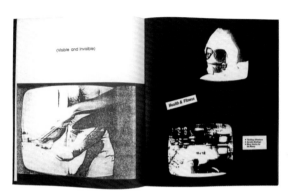

A Nuclear Atlas, 1982
SHARON GILBERT
11.5" x 9.5" Edition 500

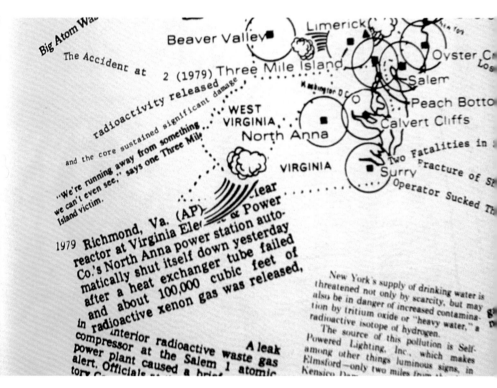

Seven Lady Saintes, 1985
ERICA VAN HORN
9.5" x 8" Edition 90

Site Readings, 1993
ANNE GEORGE
7.5" x 4.5" Edition 225

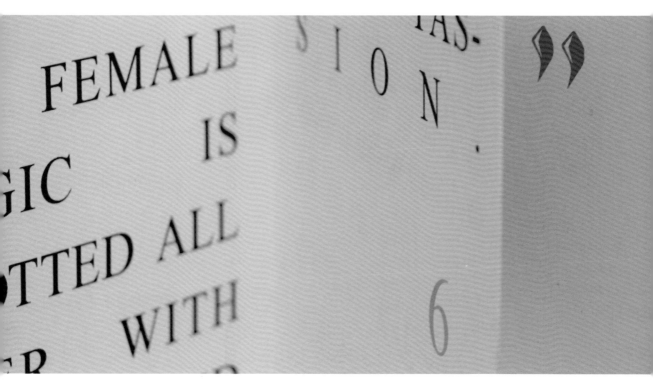

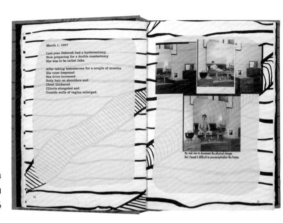

Wrongly Bodied Two, 2004
CLARISSA SLIGH
10" x 7.25" Edition 46

ng. No sad good-byes. I just want to
visibly outside who I feel like on the
king these steps, people will see what
n on the inside all my life and
dge that this is who Jake is.

ayself to look, to see as the
her, I saw my own terror,
and vulnerability when I was
eled into an operating room.
thin tubes protruded from
re Jake's breasts had been.
ned into little plastic bottles.

ing high as a kite.
not to be swallowed into

In the boldest sense I am very interested in storytelling. *Seven Lady Saintes*, the book at Women's Studio Workshop, was a very pared-down telling of each tale of each woman saint. I tried to give exactly enough information to tell the story. There aren't a lot of adjectives in there; there aren't a lot of adverbs. It's in the tradition of people like Carver and Hemingway. I feel nervous putting myself in with them. But that kind of pared down storytelling is very American.

KW: LET'S TAKE A LOOK AT SEVEN LADY SAINTES. FIRST OF ALL, IT'S CERTAINLY COMING OUT OF YOUR STUDY OF MEDIEVAL ART. AND CLEARLY YOU WERE HAVING WHAT LOOKED LIKE A KIND OF RELIGIOUS CONVERSION EXPERIENCE BECAUSE YOU DID THE SEVEN VIRTUES, AND YOU DID SEVEN LADY SAINTES. YOU'RE TALKING ABOUT THE PARED DOWN WRITING AND YET I THINK PROBABLY THE FIRST THING THAT MOST READERS AND VIEWERS OF THE BOOK WOULD COME AWAY WITH IS THE ASTONISHING COLOR; THE VISUAL QUALITY OF THE BOOK. SO IT'S INTERESTING TO HEAR YOU TALKING ABOUT IT AS A WRITTEN DOCUMENT.

Yeah, it is interesting. For me they were never separated. I had done two versions of *Seven Lady Saintes*. They were in a buckram accordion, so the whole thing was rigid. One had gray buckram and one had red. The painted versions were very, very highly colored. And when I went to do the one at the Women's Studio Workshop, I remember talking to Ann, there was X amount of money in the budget and I didn't have another penny to spend on it, so I had to exactly fit it into there. And Ann suggested that the fewer colors I used the more I could get out of my money.

KW: WE NEED TO CLARIFY THAT THIS WAS A SILKSCREEN BOOK.

This was a silkscreen book. So we reduced it. It was white paper, and we used the red and blue and black. It was reduced to three colors, which was a major shift from the way I was painting. Everything had to become a little more graphic and it was extremely exciting for me to do that kind of color separation and still to keep the patterning.

Maybe I've offended proper Catholics or maybe they don't see the humor, or maybe they think isn't this marvelous, they're portraits of these saints. It disturbed a lot of people that I was doing all this religious work when I was not religious and they thought it was a bit disrespectful because there is a humor in the way the saints are represented. But that way of bringing in humor but not a slapstick kind of humor is, I think, American.

KW: SO WHAT WAS YOUR IMPETUS TO APPLY TO THE WORKSHOP FOR A GRANT? THIS WAS 1982 OR '83, SO YOU WEREN'T REALLY A YOUNG ARTIST AT THAT POINT, WHICH WAS ONE PROFILE THAT YOU SEE QUITE A BIT AT THE WORKSHOP. AND YOU WERE IN FRANCE.

Well, there weren't very many things like that in existence and it just seemed such an amazing opportunity, to be able to go and produce a book in a place, and that you would be there specifically for that. It wouldn't be like teaching or taking a course where you're answering someone else's needs. It would be about you and your work. The other thing was that I had come from a printmaking background but ever since I'd been making books everything was one-of-a-kind. I had started thinking about the whole nature of print and getting things out in the world.

I did some books where I reduced the original, the one-of-a-kind piece, and I made it into a black-and-white version as photocopy. I'd print up ten copies and then I would come back and I'd stitch them up with my Japanese binding. And then when I traded or sold those I'd make ten more. It was a way to make an edition without having to put out a lot of money.

I made ninety copies of *Seven Lady Saintes*. That grant to go to Women's Studio gave me a chance to plan a book in a bigger edition and a more advanced version, well on from my photocopy attempts. I liked my photocopy books but, yeah, that was a big jump for me to make *Seven Lady Saintes*. And silkscreen wasn't something that I had worked in very often. I would never have planned a book in silkscreen. At the Workshop Ann really directed me, and said this is the best way we can do this. And the flatness of that color, the flatness of color for silkscreen was just perfect.

KW: DO YOU THINK IT SHIFTED YOUR IDEA THEN ABOUT EDITIONING WORK?

Absolutely, absolutely. I did come away from that wanting to do more, and then was very frustrated because I was still in this transient living stage. I was going back to Chicago, I would go back to France, I was house sitting here or doing some job, I had so many…. I was constantly moving around so I didn't have access to things like presses very often. So it wasn't easy to do something in edition. Eventually I went up to Visual Studies Workshop and did a book there. It is hard for people today to understand that when they can just print things off a desktop.

KW: SO DO YOU THINK THAT THE WORK THAT YOU DID AT THE WOMEN'S STUDIO WORKSHOP, ALTHOUGH I KNOW YOU WENT TO VISUAL STUDIES WORKSHOP A COUPLE OF YEARS LATER, FEELS LIKE IT'S A PART OF YOUR BODY OF WORK?

I think it's absolutely within my body of work and it was really a momentous thing for me because there was a distillation that happened there. I'd been already working on a distillation in my writing. The distillation within the imagery, when suddenly I couldn't use a million colors, was very interesting for me, of how to work that. Even though I might have gone back to making some more one-of-a-kind books, I was already well into a different kind of thinking, how to go about that, how to incorporate it more often or better. I'm not saying better, I think that was an extremely successful book, I'm still really proud of it.

KW: TO CONSTRUCT YOUR NARRATIVES YOU SAY THAT YOU USE 'THE PORTABILITY OF THE PRINTED SHEET.' CAN YOU EXPOUND ON THAT, ESPECIALLY IN RELATIONSHIP TO YOUR OWN WORK?

Well, as an undergraduate studying art you had to do lots of things. You had to do some sculpture, you had to learn to do metal things, and welding and stuff like that. I never liked doing things if I had to go and ask somebody to help me move it. Again, I'm quite a private person and I like being able to do it by myself. And so I liked that books are portable, and that books can go with you anywhere, you can put a paperback in your pocket, and read it on the bus or standing at the bus stop or all that. And I think when I started making books as I was traveling it became just logical that they stay small. I've made books that are twenty meters long but they always fold up, they can still go under my arm.

KW: SO THE SCALE OF YOUR WORK, WHICH OFTEN IS ON THE SMALL SIDE IS SOMETHING THAT'S QUITE INTENTIONAL ON YOUR PART.

What I'm interested in is always little detail so in a way it's sort of silly to make big books. For example, the prints on the wall behind my dining room table, the ones of the black and white dishes, those were small things, small drawings. That set of nine prints when put up on a wall like that becomes a big thing. But they also fold up, they pack up in a box, and *become* a small thing. I like that things can get bigger, they can be out in the world in a big way, and they can pack down again.

KW: YOU ALSO TALK ABOUT A DESIRE FOR YOUR WORK NOT TO BE PERFECT. CAN YOU SAY SOMETHING ABOUT THAT?

Well I'm just always a little bit not right on with my books, I'm always a little bit impatient. I think sometimes things are just made so perfect that they leave the audience outside. So *Seven Lady Saintes* is still very much made by a human being even though it was made in an edition. For example, if Ann had been doing all the printing it would have been all perfectly registered because she could do that and I just did the best I could. But I don't think there was a push from the Women's Studio that it be crafted or crafty, just that it would be the best that I could do.

DOCUMENTARY EVIDENCE:

THE AURA OF VERACITY IN ARTISTS' BOOK

JAE JENNIFER ROSSMAN   In all successful artists' books, the textual or pictorial element of the story is only a piece of the information to glean through reading. A hallmark of this medium is endowing the physical attributes of the book with part of the message. For example, in Cheri Gaulke's Impedement, created at Women's Studio Workshop in 1991, toenails are embedded into the handmade paper in this work about female shoe wear. She creates an association between the beloved and sometimes disgusting aspects of the foot. The toenail clippings allude to the dual positive/negative nature of societal fetishism of this part of the body.

Another way to add meaning through the physicality of the object is to borrow a format with which the reader is already familiar. By doing this, the artist gains an advantage: the reader brings a set of associations or assumptions and unconsciously applies them to the reading of the artist's book. The artist then has the ability to manipulate these associations that accompany a specific format.

In this essay I will look at how three artists who have been supported by the Women's Studio Workshop have used this technique of riffing on a known form of documentation. While the three artists' books I will examine make use of different formats, they all are based on the same premise: using a format that is intended to document evidence for a particular purpose. We are all familiar with these formats as part of our everyday lives: handbooks, manuals, guides, instructional booklets, even the phone book. Together these informational publications comprise an informal genre in which the compilation of facts or other forms of evidence results in the feeling of veracity of the information gathered.

1 I HAVE PREVIOUSLY ARGUED THIS POINT MORE EXTENSIVELY BY DISCUSSING THE LITERARY THEORY OF PARATEXTUAL ANALYSIS AS APPLICABLE TO ARTISTS' BOOKS. SEE *THE JOURNAL OF ARTISTS' BOOKS* 23 (SPRING 2008)

In order to better understand how the artists have employed their various chosen formats, an investigation of the physical cues outside of the main text is crucial.[1] Fully understanding what is happening physically and contextually will allow the reader to clearly understand the "how" of an artists' book since this medium aims to communicate through its form as well as its content. The textual message in addition to a clear understanding of the physical clues will enable the reader to see the "why" of the artists' book. What makes this book work? What are the component parts saying when put together? By slowly chipping away at each element of the form and the text or imagery we can accumulate a wealth of facts or clues that can be put together into a story, much like the work of an investigative reporter. For the most part, the facts are there waiting to be discovered. But the reader/reporter also needs to use his or her own cognitive abilities to put the facts/clues together to fully comprehend the whole, the overarching message.

For instance, Paula McCartney's *Bird Watching* (2006) feels rather traditional when the reader first picks it up. The boards are covered in bookcloth, quarter bound in brown with the remainder of the boards in green. The title is stamped in black on the spine and the front cover. A decorative outline of a bird is also stamped on the front cover. A small stripe of black separates the brown and green sections of the binding and contrasts with the sinuous line of the bird design. The book is approximately ten inches tall, eight inches wide, and one inch thick. It feels a bit oversized compared to the average hardcover fiction book, but the extra width and the elegant design make it feel unusual; at first glance this object reads as a well-designed trade edition. Opening the book reinforces the idea of a special trade edition: silhouetted birds flap across the light gray endsheets and a quote from John James Audubon faces the title page. Then the book presents the reader with a series of glossy color photographs of birds in a natural environment. A small amount of factual information about each bird is presented in a gridded table.

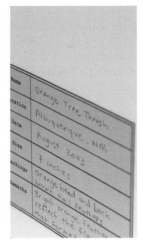

McCartney's choices of binding, size, and layout refer to both the field guide and the scientific log book. She suggests the format of a field guide by pairing documentary color photography with factual information. Field guides usually have a simplified format that allows the reader to access the necessary information to make identifications quickly while on location. As the reader looks to the information to learn more about this bird, he realizes that the facts are hand written. Additionally, the information also contains date and location information as well as personal remarks. This personal characteristic of the information refers to a log book; presumably the information is accurate, but the handwriting indicates that perhaps it is not yet public. The birds have been identified factually by name, size, and markings, but they have also been connected to the personal experience of the author. The penultimate page spread of the book provides lengthy handwritten notes about the author's bird watching experiences. The last page spread presents a diagram of the parts of a particular bird type and a map of migration patterns in the United States. The map and diagram are ways of presenting information that cement the feeling of factuality that built as the reader learned to identify a variety of bird species in their habitats. But upon closer inspection, the reader realizes the migration pattern represented is actually for the bird watcher, not the birds.

Further inspection of the photographs reveals that the birds so carefully documented are not real; they are constructions that the artist has placed in a living landscape. Once this realization is made, the feeling of veracity that the artist carefully set up is undermined. The seeming naturalism of the fake birds questions what is truly natural in today's world where the majority of us live in an environment that has been completely constructed by man. Even the seemingly natural parts of our daily existence, the trees and other plant forms, more often than not were placed in their specific location. The animals that live in the spaces constructed by man adapt to these hybrid environments. McCartney's point about the arbitrary definition of "natural" also brings to mind growing concerns about the many ways that we impose ourselves on the planet.

Classification of a Spit Stain (2000) by Ellie Ga brings to mind the laboratory journal, a form many are familiar with from high school science classes. The book is spiral bound, approximately eight-and-a-half by eleven inches, with boards covered in paper that looks like the cheap cardboard that often graces the outside of an ordinary notebook. The label on the front cover uses a typeface that reminds the reader of official forms. The title is stamped as if validating the "officialness" of the label and reinforcing the idea of a place intended to record facts. Stains on the label indicate that the notebook has been heavily used. The pages are tissue thin, "onion skin" paper alternated with thicker, three-hole-punched paper. While the reader may not have had extensive experience with this format, he understands that this is a tool used in the professional scientific community to better understand the world, the use of which can lead to "scientific breakthroughs." So not only does this format have the aura of veracity, it promises to provide groundbreaking ideas.

On the inside Ga uses a series of visual cues to reinforce the scientific feeling of the book: graph paper, checklists, charts, and photographs. Photography has a long association with veracity as photography was considered the most truthful way to capture images of the world when it was first introduced in the nineteenth century. As with McCartney, Ga's presentation of information is in a format that is associated with facts, such as charts and grids. This puts the reader in the mindset to accept what is presented as true. The artist adds a layer of official documentation with the handwritten notes, circling specific elements for identification. These notes were presumably created by a scientist, who in our culture is considered an authority. Additionally, the tone of the writing mimics the straightforward prose of scientific textbooks. But once the reader grasps the subject matter, these elements serve to accentuate the absurdity of the supposed scientific study. After the reader has been amused (or perhaps offended) by the artist's serious treatment of an often overlooked element of our daily existence, the reader may question what else he has been overlooking in the course of his day-to-day life. By paying attention to the residue of past action and the patterns that these actions form over time Ga shows the reader the beauty in banal occurrences. One might say there is a more spiritual interpretation to the work: importance found in seemingly insignificant places. Ultimately the artist has emphasized the importance of the process itself; only through the process of looking, with or without official documentation, can one find that which they seek.

Remembrance (2003) by Judith Mohns uses a portion of the obituary section as the basis for the text in this artist's book. For many, reading the newspaper is a daily experience. Scanning the pages, catching words here and there, looking for articles of interest to read in depth—there is a method to reading a newspaper that one learns almost unconsciously. Mohns emphasizes this typical newspaper reading experience of looking for bits of information by changing the tonality of some of the words on each of the book's page spreads to emphasize different aspects of the same text. The artist also sometimes enlarges a portion of the excerpted section for extra emphasis. Mohns' choice of paper, an acid-free, 100 percent recycled version of newsprint, mimics the tactile experience of reading the newspaper without sacrificing the longevity of her bookwork. However, at only six-and-a-half inches square the size of this book makes a distinct break with the often awkward experience of reading the much larger standard newspaper format. No folding is needed for the reader to interact comfortably with Mohns' work. The small format emphasizes that only a portion of the newspaper's text was excerpted, thus encouraging the reader to think about not only the text in this book, but that which was not included. A single signature pamphlet stitch binding with natural linen thread secures the pages of the bookwork without veering too far from the stacked and folded pages of the newspaper which it suggests.

On the immediate level, this is a book about remembering the deceased, those we knew and those we did not. Mohns' visual emphasis centers around the various roles these people played in their lives as individuals, parts of families, workers, and other contributors to society. How does one determine what was the most important role or roles? What should be included in this notice that attempts to sum up an entire life? While reflecting on how these people were remembered, the reader likely ponders how he or she will be remembered. What will my obituary say? And why do we feel the need to share with the newspaper audience that this person has passed on and what his or her life entailed? As with so many rituals around death, this practice is really for the living. While this book makes the reader pose many questions around the practice of reading the obituary page, the artist is also exploring the practice of reading on a broader level. Presenting the same text repeatedly, but in visually diverse ways, forces the reader to interact with the text in a different way each time. Eventually the reader can draw a parallel between the societally taught practice of the obituary page and the ways that society influences one's reading practices and habits.

Ultimately all artists' books are about reading. Our interaction with a book is based on our knowledge of reading practices. We may not always try to read a book in the straightforward, cover-to-cover, in-page-order way we were taught in school. Yet, we do employ some reading strategy that we have learned through interacting with books. We attempt to use those same reading strategies when interacting with artists' books, but the artists have purposefully interfered with our ability to approach the book in our typical manner. Sometimes this interference is extremely subtle, but it always exists in a successful artist's book. In the examples above, the artists are playing with the aura of veracity that the reader associates with certain informational formats. Adding this to the aura of authenticity that already exists around an art object heightens the intensity of "truth" of what the artist presents. Even when the idea of veracity is not directly addressed in an artist's book, it is still there because as readers we are taught that books present information that can be considered factual or truthful—not in the sense of non-fiction, but in the sense of the integrity of the information. The everyday associations of the book are combined with the associations of the more rarified art object resulting in a variety of layers that can be manipulated by the artist. It is these layers that make artists' books a unique and powerful format.

JAE JENNIFER ROSSMAN IS THE ASSISTANT DIRECTOR FOR SPECIAL COLLECTIONS AT THE ROBERT B. HAAS FAMILY ARTS LIBRARY, YALE UNIVERSITY.

WOMEN ART FOOD

MARY-KAY LOMBINO In *Art Life Food: Potluck Recipes from Women's Studio Workshop*, published in 2009 to commemorate their 35th anniversary, the founders of the Workshop open with the statement that artists come to the studio for the art but they stay for the food. The truth and humor of this statement epitomizes the close relationship that food and art share in the hearts and minds of the many participants who have come to make art at this mostly female, domestic-scaled workspace over the years. The book cleverly divides the recipes into categories such as *Green, Glorious Green and Purple! Red! Magenta!* named more for their aesthetic similarities than their culinary connections. Additional sections on *Life Recipes* (with notes on lipstick application for non-smearing, schmoozing, and noshing by Barbara Leoff Burge) and *Studio Recipes* (with practical instructions for making paper clay, play dough, and salt dough for making holiday crafts) serve as delightful reminders that this is, for the most part, written by and for women artists. Much of the text and images are presented with a certain knowing wit that speaks to the camaraderie or sisterhood in the making of the book that is reminiscent of the early years of the feminist art movement, which took hold not long before the Women's Studio Workshop was founded.

The Feminist Art Program, founded by Judy Chicago first in Fresno, California, and in 1971 with Miriam Schapiro at the California Institute of the Arts near Los Angeles, became known for artistic collaboration. Making art collaboratively was often a way of challenging the myth of solitary (male) creative genius. However, making this comparison is not to say that the Women's Studio Workshop is simply a seventies throwback environment where outdated notions of female essentialism are recycled. To the contrary, the studio is a site for inspiration, innovation, and the development of new ideas, methods, and forms, bringing new life to such subjects as stereotypical symbols of women's identity as nurturers and sex objects. For example, three of the artists who have taken residence at the Women's Studio Workshop, Katherine Aoki, Susan Baker, and Diane Jacobs, have created artists' books that address the topic of female sexuality as humorous metaphors for serving and consuming food.

Aoki's *How I Lost My Vegetarianism* (1998) is a thin sewn book, which features a collection of fourteen anecdotes, illustrated with screen prints, from vegetarian and ex-vegetarian women who struggle with their relationship to meat. The title is a play on words that recalls the more commonly heard, "How I lost my virginity" stories that might be told among a tightly knit group of women over drinks or on a date as a way of getting to know a potential sex partner. The individual narratives further imply the metaphor by making references to temptation, drinking, peer pressure, and regret, all of which draw obvious parallels to youthful first sexual encounters. In one example the text reads, "I was infatuated with this guy. During a date we went to a fast food place. I thought, 'This guy is kind of cute; I think I'll have a hamburger.' It was really quite lame." The accompanying image shows a french-fry carton overturned with the fries cascading out and a soda cup with its straw bent down like a mournful head bowing down in regret. In the image, the burger is gone (presumably already consumed) and the fries are spilled—a subtle message is relayed that there is no going back. In another scenario the narrator reveals, "I was in a bar in St. Louis with a bunch of guys. They ordered Buffalo wings without asking me. I was bored and ate one without thinking twice." Below the text is a wonderfully detailed image of two buffalo that seem to sneakily blend into the wood grain of the side of a bar as though they are the culprits lurking near the scene of the crime. The dark, bulky silhouettes of the buffalo can be seen as stand-ins for lecherous male predators waiting around the bar for the unsuspecting female.

In both of these examples, as well as with the others collected in Aoki's book, the female eater does not appear in the images. Instead, Aoki presents a whimsical sketch on each page of the offending food (or what's left of it) or alternatively the setting in which it was consumed, leaving the image of the woman's body, and the act of eating, up to the viewer's imagination. The absence of the female figure revamps the feminist approach to challenging the male gaze by "taking back" representations of the female body. One of the central issues addressed by Judy Chicago and other artists involved with the Feminist Art Program was the way in which Western art and other avenues of visual culture such as advertising traditionally represented the female body as an object of male desire. This led to a proliferation of images of female body parts depicted by women both literally and metaphorically such as in Chicago's *The Dinner Party* (1979), a monumental installation meant to reinsert great women that were "consumed by history" back into the collective memory of Western Civilization. Chicago's work, along with other feminist art from that period, has been widely criticized for attempting to define the essence of the universal female experience. Aoki not only avoids the potentially essentializing act of depicting women, she also gives each of the female narrators a chance to tell her own story. And perhaps more importantly, she positions women not as objects of male desire but as subjects with their own desires that are often too powerful to resist.

Don't Bug the Waitress (1987) by Susan Baker is not a traditional book but a bright blue, three-paneled pocket folder made to recall a café menu. In each pocket is a sheet folded as an accordion with humorous anecdotes and colorful silkscreen images that visually and verbally describe the plight of a waitress told from behind the scenes. The center pocket reads, "a waitress is half way between a shrink and a hooker." The slogan is a telling comment on the psychological and sexual expectations that come with the act of a woman serving food to strangers. Even in this lighthearted, tongue-in-cheek remark Baker engages in another of the central activities of the Feminist Art Program, which was to discover a common oppression based on gender, which came to define roles and identities of women. The feminist artists of the early 1970s, through consciousness-raising sessions in which they examined their personal experiences, analyzed the social and political mechanisms of this oppression, thus placing their personal histories into a larger cultural perspective. This was the direct application of the slogan of 1970s feminism: The personal is political.

Baker divulges another occupational hazard: what the artist calls "waitress disease —the blotch on the breast" in an image showing a woman with a look of anguish on her bright pink face as she carries five plates, one of which is pressed against her breast, now smeared with food. In the background are three irate men, each making a different proprietary gesture towards her as she makes her way through another tough day on the job. Even when dished out in Baker's cartoon-like style with a large dose of humor, the image of the woman's food-stained breast serves as a symbol of the lack of dignity in playing the role of servant and locates sexual issues within the larger context of identity, intimacy, and power. Baker's work brings to mind *Nurturant Kitchen* by Susan Frazier, Vicki Hodgetts, and Robin Weltsch, one of several installations in *Womanhouse*, a large-scale cooperative project executed by the students in the Feminist Art Program in 1972. The artists transformed the actual former kitchen of the house by painting the walls lipstick pink and covering them with foam fried eggs that gradually transformed into sagging breasts, a metaphor for the burden of perpetually feeding and nurturing others. Both *Nurturant Kitchen* and *Don't Bug the Waitress* can be seen as metaphors for the exhaustion and degradation of women trapped in selfless service to others. However, the dramatic power employed in the *Womanhouse* installation has been replaced by Baker's biting sarcasm and the intimacy of an artist's book. This medium allows the artist to deliver her message, not as a grand statement of protest, but instead like a private joke jotted down on a napkin and passed on to a friend.

In *Alphabet Tricks* (2000), Diane Jacobs uses the intimacy of the book as well as a critique of patriarchal language to expose society's objectification of female sexuality. The small black book is contained in a red linen slipcase and unfolds like a delicate accordion. Each page reveals a carefully sewn, translucent paper pocket with a silkscreen illustration. Partially hidden inside each pocket is a card printed with a corresponding definition in large, bold type and a tiny red sentence using the word along the top edge of the card. As the reader makes his or her way through the alphabet, it quickly becomes apparent that the definitions are derogatory labels that position women as objects of desire, ridicule, property, or some form of degradation. Several of the words, including *beef, cherry, dish, jelly,* and *milkshake,* relate the female body to food. The artist attempts to present a report of such deprecating, gender-coded comparisons while working within the prescribed format of the dictionary.

One historical use of text to expose gender inequities and stereotypes in society is exemplified in the work of the Guerrilla Girls. This anonymous group of feminist artists established in the 1980s in New York has a talent for fitting biting criticism with just the right format to deliver powerful messages with a sense of humor, frankness, and authority. The *Guerrilla Girls' Pop Quiz* poster, for instance, asks, "If February is Black History Month and March is Women's History Month, what happens the rest of the year?" Their answer, which appears upside-down below, is simply put and packs a punch: *discrimination.* The posters, mass-produced and plastered on everything from the backs of city busses to the inside of public bathroom stalls, are ephemera rather than treasured objects intended to last.

By contrast, in *Alphabet Tricks,* the craftsmanship and attention to detail required to create this object are exemplary. It is a beautifully designed, almost precious object meant to be held and manipulated with the utmost of care. However, when compared to the persuasiveness of the Guerrilla Girls' posters, Jacobs' use of text is sometimes an inconsistent fusion of dictionary-speak and slang that results in lengthy, awkward prose. For instance, the definition for *cherry* reads as follows: "The uneaten fruit of a female, ranging in color from pale pink to deep red or blackish, belonging to any of several varieties, including some cultivated for their fruits or ornamental flowers." And the page for *dish* is even less clear: "A woman prepared in a particularly attractive way; usu. shallow and able to hold various quantities." The artist, in trying to stay true to the form of a dictionary and remain subtle in her critique, misses the opportunity for a more pointed, perhaps humorous commentary on the deep-seeded chauvinism that is embedded in daily speech. However, like Baker's *Don't Bug the Waitress* and Aoki's *How I Lost My Vegetarianism,* this lovely book does possess a sense of woman-to-woman intimacy in the act of revealing each page as the book unfolds and an appreciation for the hand made. These three books also share with many of the other books created at the Women's Studio Workshop a form of feminist critique that is more subtle, unassuming, and perhaps more humble than its predecessors.

Judith Stein wrote in *The Power of Feminist Art* that women artists in the early period of the movement "took inspiration from the format of the potluck supper, where each guest contributes a culinary creation for the common good, the meal as a whole being greater than the sum of its parts."[1] This is a fitting metaphor for the Women's Studio Workshop, the site for daily real-life potluck lunches and hub of creative collaboration. The studio is a product of the 1970s, a period that saw the renewal of feminism in America when artistic collaboration became for many women a political act. Today, the personal voice, rather than the political, has become a creative first choice and a key component of the collective output of the studio.

1 NORMA BROUDE AND MARY D. GARRARD, *THE POWER OF FEMINIST ART: THE AMERICAN MOVEMENT OF THE 1970S HISTORY AND IMPACT.* HARRY N. ABRAMS, SEPTEMBER 1, 1996, P. 228.

MARY-KAY LOMBINO IS THE CURATOR IN CHARGE OF CONTEMPORARY ART AND PHOTOGRAPHY AT THE FRANCES LEHMAN LOEB ART CENTER AT VASSAR COLLEGE

BUILDING A REPOSITORY
OF ARTISTS' BOOKS
FROM WOMEN'S STUDIO WORKSHOP

RONALD PATKUS

"The space of a book is intimate and public at the same time; it mediates between private reflection and broad communication in a way that matches many women's lived experience."

—Johanna Drucker, in
The Book as Art (2007)

According to the *American Library Association Glossary*, a repository is "a place where archives, manuscripts, books, or other documents are stored." The glossary further notes that the term is frequently used synonymously with "depository," though both terms are distinct from "depository library," which refers to a library legally designated to collect publications produced by federal or state agencies. Does this mean that all libraries are repositories? Well, yes, in a certain way, but in practice people often use the term to refer to an institution that documents a specific topic in depth (perhaps one among many). Thus some libraries are repositories of the papers and/or publications of a particular author or organization. Today many libraries are interested in building "institutional repositories," which are online sites that seek to collect and provide access to an institution's intellectual output.

A number of libraries and institutions in the United States have collected artists' books from the Women's Studio Workshop (WSW), which today functions as the largest producer of such books in the country. Six in particular, though, have made commitments to document fully the output of the organization. They include five universities (University of Delaware, Indiana University, Virginia Commonwealth University, Yale University, Rochester Institute of Technology) and one college, Vassar College. The decision made by any academic institution to serve as a repository is based on numerous factors unique to that institution, and is reached after careful consideration. It also reflects a two-sided commitment, on the part of both producer and receiver, to preserve WSW books. This is certainly true in Vassar's case, where a repository was established in 2007.

I first learned about WSW in the spring of 2006, when I was co-teaching a course titled *The Medium of Print and the History of Books*. Professor of English Robert DeMaria and I approach this course in a roughly chronological fashion, and we were looking for a way to consider artists' books at the end of the semester. I began to hear about the work of the WSW, and eventually contacted the director, Ann Kalmbach. We had a couple of exchanges, and made plans for me to bring the class to the Workshop. This visit was a great success, opening new worlds to the students. They were especially intrigued to see the way materials and ideas came together in the various books by artists. It was also important for them to see the space itself; many students saw presses and other printing equipment and supplies for the first time. Needless to say, the visit added a great dimension to our discussion of artists' books. Ann and Artistic Director Tatana Kellner subsequently visited Vassar to give presentations on the WSW books to other classes.

In 2007 Vassar and WSW began to talk about the possibility of the college becoming an official repository of the works created by WSW artists. The two institutions reached an agreement whereby the library would acquire all books produced before 2007 over a five-year period (i.e. by 2011), and would also commit to the ongoing acquisition of future books. The agreement thus solidified an existing relationship, but also moved it forward in a significant way. Though several other institutions had already become repositories, there were still good reasons for Vassar and WSW to come together.

A first and obvious connection was concern for women and their work in the world. Vassar was founded in 1861 by Poughkeepsie philanthropist Matthew Vassar to create the first "fully endowed institution for the education of women." In the years that followed, the institution emerged as a leading center of higher learning, one which prepared many women for significant careers in a variety of fields. The college became co-educational in 1969 and entered a new stage of development, but Vassar still retains a strong sense of its history and commitment to issues important to women. The WSW, for its part, has women's issues at the core of its mission. Since its establishment in 1974 by Ann Kalmbach, Tatana Kellner, Anita Wetzel, and Barbara Leoff Burge, it has functioned as an alternative space for women artists, one where books are created that reflect the social and political concerns of women in recent decades.

Another connection between Vassar and WSW is an interest in books and the book arts. Vassar faculty early on adopted pedagogical principles based on the use of primary sources in the classroom. It was the first college founded with an original art collection and gallery, and the library developed related holdings. Early in the twentieth century, legendary librarians like Dorothy Plum formed ties with publisher Mitchell Kennerley and printer Frederic Goudy of the Village Press; today Vassar holds some of the country's finest holdings of these key figures. The library continues this interest in the book arts by maintaining relationships with artists, presses, and organizations in the Hudson Valley. WSW engages in multiple artistic endeavors; it describes itself as "a visual arts organization with specialized studios in printmaking, hand papermaking, ceramics, letterpress printing, photography, and the book arts." Artists' books are a central focus, though, and since 1979 it has produced about 180 such books, testifying to its important place in the book arts community.

Vassar and WSW also have in common a strong interest in the Hudson Valley and its constituent communities. Vassar's president Catharine Hill has made a priority of working with the local community. Through the college's field work program, students and faculty interact with local agencies and organizations, for instance, and the annual Community Works Campaign provides financial support to local groups. From its founding in 1974, WSW has been a part of the local community. Its location in a historic building in Rosendale, New York, and its ties with community members keep it grounded in the Hudson Valley, even as it develops a national and international reputation.

For all of these reasons—a connection to women, an interest in the book arts, and a commitment to working with local communities—Vassar was a logical choice to serve as a repository for WSW. WSW gains another stable site for the preservation of the artists' books that are created under its auspices, while Vassar further develops its library holdings in an area that has long been a collecting interest. These benefits are important, but the building of a repository perhaps has greatest value when it reaches further.

In a short period of time, the Vassar-WSW agreement has encouraged new activities and new collaborations. With a substantial number of WSW artists' books in the Vassar collection, students quickly became interested in researching individual artists and the WSW as an organization. A number of students have written papers in succeeding iterations of the *History of the Book* course, and in other courses. Moreover, the presence of the WSW collection has now led to the establishment of a new course which will be offered at Vassar in the spring of 2011 by Professor Lisa Collins and Art Center curator Mary-Kay Lombino. Titled *Artists' Books from the Women's Studio Workshop,* and cross-listed through the Art Department and the Women's Studies Program, this seminar will meet in the Archives and Special Collections Library and draw heavily on WSW books. The repository is therefore clearly supporting the curriculum in multiple ways, the ideal result of any collection development endeavor at an educational institution. The exhibition *Hand, Voice & Vision: Artists' Books from Women's Studio Workshop* and this, its accompanying catalog, also exemplify the collaborations that proceed from the existence of this repository. Vassar helped secure funding for the exhibition, and its curators have been involved in the production of the catalog. A version of the exhibition will be on view at Vassar in 2012.

In a certain sense, one may see a repository as an internally-focused endeavor: materials are collected, cataloged, and preserved in order to build that special place where books are stored. This is a traditional but important function, for libraries still are distinguished by the wealth of their collections. But I think it is fair to say that just as artists' books have both private and public dimensions (as insightfully noted by Johanna Drucker in the excerpt at the beginning of this essay), so, too,

RONALD PATKUS IS HEAD OF SPECIAL COLLECTIONS AND ADJUNCT ASSOCIATE PROFESSOR OF HISTORY AT VASSAR COLLEGE. can organizations that support their creation, and institutions that house them. WSW provides an alternative space where women can work, while also sharing and celebrating this work. The Vassar repository reaches its fullest potential not just through collecting, but also by creating and realizing possibilities for teaching, research, and ongoing collaboration.

ARTISTS' BOOKS FROM
WOMEN'S STUDIO WORKSHOP:
THE ART MUSEUM PERSPECTIVE

they creak, hiss, and whine

Artists' books—including Women's Studio Workshop (WSW) publications—are understood as works of art offering an approach to form and content within the context of a book. Frequently acting as signposts or messengers, artists' books often focus on issues of importance to society including conflict, the environment, gender, politics, and race. Personal topics abound, ranging from love to loss, often presented in an imaginative way utilizing the intimate qualities of the book format.

DEIRDRE E. LAWRENCE

"WSW books have to have a life after the studio."
—Tatana Kellner interview, April 12, 2010.

WSW is known as a place where artists work in a varied range of media, which begs the question as to why an artist chooses the book form as their palette or medium, instead of selecting another format such as a painting, photograph, print, or sculpture. Very often it is the physical attribute of the book that appeals to the artist (as well as the viewer/reader), offering intimacy in a one-to-one relationship. The sequential elements of a book result in a dynamic interaction with the viewer and the book format offers portability and accessibility on an intimate level. Indeed the structural book form moves beyond being a platform for text and images and is a vehicle of communication within itself. The book form offers a viewer/reader an experience that is both tactile and visual and involves hands-on engagement that is not possible with other media such as painting or sculpture.

Artists' books within an institutional setting, such as a museum, present a challenge in terms of display and issues of security versus access. Security rules often inhibit the possibility of a physical engagement with the book. When a book is presented in a locked case the viewer can only see select pages, without the opportunity to see other pages or hold the entire book. Clearly vitrines or locked display cases are not conducive to the viewer/participant experience. Other options include scanning pages into a software program so that the entire book can be viewed on a screen, or displaying page proofs on the wall, repeating the sequence in which the pages appear in the book. While providing greater access, these techniques do not reproduce the tactile experience the viewer has when handling an artist's book. Of course, one could just put a copy of a book out for total viewing with a second copy in the wings in case of damage or loss. This is an expensive option for many institutions since artists' books can sell for hundreds of dollars. More options for display techniques are needed so that museums and other institutions can showcase artists' books while still providing access and protecting the object, so these works of art can be experienced in the manner that the artist intended.

So now let's focus specifically on artists' books created by the Women's Studio Workshop. Since 1979, WSW has produced more than 180 artists' books by providing a nesting place for advice and creation and a distribution point for artists and their work. WSW books cover a wide array of subjects created by a diverse group of artists. Form and content receive equal attention, with collaborative decisions made about every aspect of the book, including the choice of paper, type of binding, printing, typography, and design. The resulting books are excellent examples of printing techniques including intaglio, letterpress and screen printing, photographic processes, and digital technologies, as well as different approaches to binding, including sculptural forms, challenging the traditional codex format. These absorbing books delight the senses and offer opportunities for reflection and intellectual stimulation. When opened, each book delivers a compelling viewer participant experience.

Where do WSW books go after they are published? Many are collected by libraries—academic, public, and museum—and by individual collectors. A recent search for WSW publications in WorldCat, a union catalog recording the collections of libraries around the world, provides insight into what is held by art museum libraries. According to WorldCat, the largest holder of WSW publications is the Museum of Modern Art (MoMA) Library, with more than fifty titles. Next is the Brooklyn Museum Library, followed by the Library at the Getty Research Institute, the Clark Art Institute Library, the libraries of the Museum of Fine Arts in Boston and the Albright-Knox Art Gallery. (This survey does not reflect libraries which do not contribute their holdings to WorldCat or print departments in institutions which generally do not record their holdings in library databases.)

Aside from collecting, several museums, art centers, and galleries have featured WSW books in their exhibitions and public programs. These include the Center for Book Arts in New York, the Islip Art Museum, the Hessisches Landesmuseum in Darmstadt, Germany, the Robert C. Williams Paper Museum, and Yale University, as well as the Brooklyn Museum. Some recent exhibitions that have included WSW books are *Beyond the Text: Artists' Books from the Collection of Robert J. Ruben*, held at The Grolier Club, *Fit to Be Bound*, held at the Everson Museum of Art, *Book is a book is a book or is it?* at the Free Library of Philadelphia, and *Social Remarques* at The University of the Arts in Philadelphia.

Begun in the 1970s, the Brooklyn Museum Library Artist's Book Collection has approximately 3,000 volumes covering the full range of artists' books from multiples to limited editions to unique bookworks. Being in New York City, we have the opportunity to build a collection that complements other larger artists' books collections such as those in the MoMA and the New York Public Library. We have developed a collection policy that does not define what an artist's book is but instead allows for the acquisition of all types of books that are defined by artists as falling under the term artists' books. The Brooklyn Museum collects both traditional and non-traditional book formats with a goal to acquire a full range of imaginative and innovative examples of the artist's book.

The collecting focus at the Brooklyn Museum is broken into four categories that often intersect. The Museum Library collects works by the following:

* artists who are considered to be innovators or masters in the artist's book world

* artists who are exhibited by the Museum or who have work in the Museum's object collection

* artists who create work that relates to the objects or cultures that are represented in the Museum's object collections

* artists who work or live in Brooklyn

The Brooklyn Museum Library owns several artists' books published by WSW, starting with *4 x 4* published in 1981 and created by Workshop founders Barbara Leoff Burge, Ann Kalmbach, Tatana Kellner, and Anita Wetzel. The following are descriptions of four additional WSW artists' books in the Library collection that reflect the collecting range:

A Nuclear Atlas by Sharon Gilbert (1944–2005) WSW, 1982. Edition of 500. Offset lithography.

Sharon Gilbert's masterwork of collages is culled from maps, facts and statistics concerning nuclear sites and accidents. Published after Three Mile Island but before Chernobyl, the book is a visual presentation of collaged information resembling concrete poetry presenting ugly information in a very beautiful way. Sharon Gilbert was a Brooklyn-based artist who worked in several media; this book is one of twelve books by Gilbert in the Artists' Book collection here. This work is an excellent example of political messaging encapsulated in a powerful visual presentation in a very simple format.

In Sharon Gilbert's words:

My work incorporates the language of media, science and statistical jargon. I attempt to make more visible issues of public significance...My method is simply to gather and isolate fragments or bits of events, as a reminder for the future.[2]

2 ARTIST'S STATEMENT FROM THE SHARON GILBERT ARTIST'S FILE, BROOKLYN MUSEUM LIBRARY.

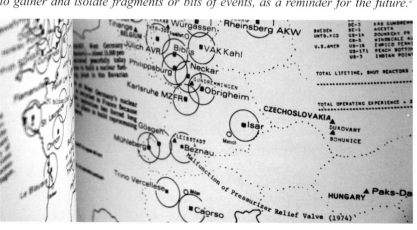

Crazy Quilt by Maureen Cummins (1963–) New York: WSW and Inanna Press, 1998. printed at the Women's Studio Workshop. Number 5 of edition of 100. Silkscreen and letterpress on cover-stock paper. Binding consists of cloth over boards and hinged pages unfolding in four directions.

An imaginative use of text against fields of color and patterns, this work presents excerpts of writings by women who were institutionalized for insanity, in a form resembling a Victorian quilt. I chose to include this book in the Artists' Book exhibition held at the Brooklyn Museum in 2000 because of its strong visual and intellectual content. Maureen Cummins summed up the book well in the exhibition catalog:

Crazy Quilt assembles the experiences of women imprisoned for madness over the last century, from the Civil War to the present, and features unknown women as well as celebrated figures such as Kate Millett. Each page is a patchwork of black alternating with rich blocks of color; text is in the form of stitch-like handwriting. The hinged pages unfold in four directions, resembling a crazy quilt.[3]

Forgotten Knowledge by Marisol Limon Martinez, WSW, 2002, Number 31 of an edition of 50. Spiral bound, silkscreen and Xerox with various kinds of paper. Purchased with funds donated by Anita Grossman Solomon in memory of her husband, Horace.

Text and images dance on these pages that illuminate a meditation on family, home, life, and loss. The interaction of text and images is printed in a style that jumps off the pages as the viewer travels from cover to cover.

This book is a visual attempt to piece together my great-grandmother's enigmatic life between Mexico and the United States. It was assembled by combining different words, documents, images, photographs, geometry, dreams, & icons.[4]

3 P. 20 FROM *ARTISTS BOOKS* (BROOKLYN MUSEUM, 2000)

4 ARTIST'S STATEMENT FROM WEBSITE: HTTP://MLIMONMARTINEZART.COM/ARTWORK/1305385_FORGOTTEN_KNOWLEDGE_LA_FLOR.HTML. FOR MORE INFORMATION ON BROOKLYN'S COLLECTION SEE: LAWRENCE, DEIRDRE E. ARTISTS BOOKS (BROOKLYN MUSEUM OF ART, 2000) "CULTURAL SIGNPOSTS: ART AND TEXT TOGETHER THROUGH THE AGES" IN *ARTEXTS* (JAMAICA CENTER FOR ARTS & LEARNING, 2001)

"ARTISTS' BOOKS AT THE BROOKLYN MUSEUM OF ART" IN THE *ARTISTS' BOOK YEARBOOK* 2001–2002 (IMPACT PRESS AT THE CENTRE FOR FINE PRINT RESEARCH, 2001)

Patterned Pleasures by Amanda Kalinoski, WSW, 2009, edition of 50. Silkscreen and letterpress with typewritten text. Original text by Carrie Hempfer. Purchased with funds donated by Mary B. Dorward.

Patterned Pleasures explores the beauty of mating rituals of humans and animals. In this concertina-fold book, text and images are interwoven to reveal a dialogue about sexuality. Kalinoski's experience with fabric is apparent as she entices the viewer with patterns into the framework of the book only to discover the subject matter. Similar to the books discussed above, this book is an excellent example of how text and images can pull a viewer into the book and then become involved with the topic at hand.

All these books—with well-integrated text and images—visually present ideas of relevance to a large and varied audience. The books fit well into the Museum's overall encyclopedic collection, ranging from antiquity to contemporary art, and touch upon history or ideas that resonate with other objects in the collection. They are also innovative examples of book art and printing which carry on the Museum's history of showcasing these traditions in its collecting and exhibition history. Exhibition opportunities at the Museum include the Elizabeth A. Sackler Center for Feminist Art, featuring work by women artists, as well as the frequently updated Contemporary Art Galleries. WSW books, as well as other artists' books, are frequently exhibited in the Library Display Cases and are viewed by visiting artists, students, and scholars. Images from the artist's book collection are included on the Museum's website and blogs often feature the artist's book collection to introduce these books to a larger audience worldwide.

WSW has commissioned works that constitute a critical mass of artists' books, many of which contribute to the understanding of our changing society. These books play a key role in contemporary art today and should be integrated into the mainstream and showcased by art museums in their main exhibition displays on a permanent basis.

DEIRDRE LAWRENCE, PRINCIPAL LIBRARIAN AT THE BROOKLYN MUSEUM, HAS AUTHORED SEVERAL ESSAYS AND ORGANIZED MANY EXHIBITIONS ABOUT ARTISTS' BOOKS INCLUDING ARTISTS BOOKS (2000).

DIMENSIONS IN ACCESS

THE DIGITAL ARTISTS' BOOK ARCHIVE OF

WOMEN'S STUDIO WORKSHOP

SYLVIA TURCHYN From the publication of its first artist's book in 1979 until 2001 the Women's Studio Workshop had amassed a formidable publication catalog of more than 125 limited-edition handmade artists' books. Of those titles circa thirty-four percent were out-of-print, making those works of art available only to patrons of special collections in libraries, museums, and archives or to the private collector. The twenty-two-year hallmark of publishing in 2001 proved to be a catalyst for redefinition and expansion of the Workshop's role in promoting visual arts. Tatana Kellner, co-founder and artistic director, envisioned the creation of an online archive of out-of-print artists' books as a featured part of the Workshop's presence on the Web. Through a successful grant application, funding for this project was provided by the New York State Council on the Arts.

Based on a recommendation from mutual colleague B.J. Irvine, then head of the Indiana University Fine Arts Library on the Bloomington campus, Kellner inquired if I would be interested in creating "cataloging-like" descriptions for the artists' books. I was intrigued by the offer, having trained the catalogers of this genre for the extensive collection at the aforementioned Fine Arts Library, and so I readily agreed.

It was never the intent of the Workshop to create digital manifestations that would be equal to or function as adequate replacements for the artists' books. Rather, the books would remain as the primary source material, with both the scanned images and accompanying book descriptions serving as surrogates to facilitate research and other educational endeavors. When data elements were developed and defined for the book descriptions no attributes were assigned to the artist's book as a digital object. All cataloging described the tangible artist's book, not its virtual facsimile. After securing permission from the book artists to display their works online, digital image files for all of the artists' books published at the Workshop were created. Any textual content in an artist's book was only readable if it was large enough to be identified as such in the online display. Every page of the out-of-print editions was made available on the digital archive while select representative pages of the in-print collections were viewable.

While creating an online archive was the primary goal of this project, of equal status was the need for an inventory and sales management system at the Workshop. Software packages or file programs that supported one activity did not adequately maintain the other. Consequently, the two virtual processes remain essentially separated to this day. Artists' books published by the Workshop were always available for purchase at the Workshop but now this process would be expanded to the Web via an online book purchasing option integrated with the archive data.

In June 2002 I spent one week on site, developing a database of descriptive elements (metadata) in collaboration with Kellner and other Workshop staff. At least one archival copy of each artist's book published by the WSW is maintained on site. This initial version, which was built with spreadsheet software, contained many of the common core elements found in a library catalog: creator (author/artist), other contributor, title, alternate title, date, paging, dimensions, other publishing information, and ISBN. A signature field was also included and noted when a title was "signed by the artist." Subject elements, referencing the topic or contents of the artists' books, were applied rarely. Because of the nature of the collection and the opportunity to create a customized database, we agreed to define and include numerous additional elements that would address the mixed-media nature of artists' books. Those notes included the following categories: printing method, binding, structure, typeface, and paper.

When describing the initial version of this archive it is important to highlight the other distinguishing features that were included in the database at the onset. Every book in the archive is accompanied by a description prepared by the artist which is then featured in the database. These narratives offer unique conceptual and contextual detail, provided in the artist's own words. A separate note element listing the funding agencies affiliated with the creation of each title is also a unique feature of the database. With the ability of artists to realize the creation of artists' books so intrinsically linked to the generosity of funding organizations, it makes good sense to acknowledge that key part of the process. The presence of this information also serves as a constant reminder to those searching the database of the crucial partnership that financial support provides the arts. Finally, every described book carries a listing of each institution that has added that artist's book to its collection. Labeled in the database as "holdings", the commonly used term in libraries, this cumulative list encompasses 198 domestic and international libraries and cultural centers. A further analysis by type reveals the following distribution of WSW titles:

University and research libraries	44%
College libraries	21%
Museums and archives	13%
Institutes, centers and schools	10%
Public libraries	7%
Foreign collections	5%

In 2002-03 I continued to build the archive database with the emphasis shifting to the initial backlog of in-print artists' books. Once those titles were described I continued to add prospective publications to the growing database as they were announced. During that era the initial plan to limit viewing of the complete contents of artists' books to out-of-print editions was revisited. Recognizing the potential research and educational value of providing full image and text files for all artists' books, the Workshop directors decided to expose the complete digital content to all artists' books they publish. The fully digitized artists' books are available in portable document file format from the Workshop's archive web page (www.wsworkshop.org) in the Artists' Books Archive section.

In 2005 Ann Kalmbach, WSW executive director, Kellner and I met in Indiana to perform a systematic review of our joint design of the initial database. After three years of active development of the archive it was an appropriate time to perform a complete analysis and plan for improvements. Another compelling catalyst was Johanna Drucker's article "Critical issues / exemplary works" (Bonefolder 1, no. 2 (Spring 2005), http://www.philobiblon.com/bonefolder/vollno2contents.htm, in which she outlined a complex metadata standard for a proposed artists' books database. While not suitable for the WSW goals and intent, the list of fields in this proposal proved useful as a comparative tool for our review. From that exercise we added the following elements to the core list of fields:

Writer	Creator of the text-based content; artist may hold multiple functions
Printer	Artist may hold multiple functions
Binder	Artist may hold multiple functions
Genre	One or more of the following controlled terms: poem, short story, diary, graphic novel, personal narrative, documentary
Copyright Owner	Artist may hold multiple functions
Source	One or more of the following controlled terms: Appropriated images, appropriated text, found images, found text

Within the process of this review we also corrected some early decisions that would limit the usefulness of this database as a searchable resource beyond the context of the Women's Studio Workshop. By adding a publisher field the formal name of the Workshop would be a searchable term within the database. I also implemented the systematic use of the following content in the subject field: Artists' books—Specimen. Based on the Library of Congress' assigned subject for this art form, this controlled term supports the customized searching of this type of material in a broader Web environment. A grant from the New York State Council on the Arts funded the expansion of the database and the migration to an open-source database software, which presented a greater ease of data entry, management, searching, and display.

WOMEN'S STUDIO WORKSHOP ARTIST'S BOOK DETAILS

Title:	How to eat your enemy
Creator:	Claire Rau
Description:	*How to Eat Your Enemy* is based on a 14th century Richard Coeur de Lion crusading manuscript and the infamous card deck from the Iraq war. Portraits of terrorists from the FBI Most Wanted Terrorist web site stare at the reader, while the recto side recounts King Richard's apparent taste for the enemy flesh.
Paging:	[17] p.
Dimensions:	69 x 70 cm. folded to 23 x 22.5 cm.
Date:	2006
Publisher:	Women's Studio Workshop
Copyright Owner:	Claire Rau
Edition:	25
ISBN:	1893125491
Printing Method:	Letterpress, Screenprint
Binding:	Handmade slipcase
Structure:	Fold book
Typeface:	Caslon
Paper:	Arches 88
Funding Source:	New York State Council on the Arts
Other Notes:	Text translated and derived from 14th century manuscript by Leona F. Cordery
Other Notes:	3 bi-fold panels hinged to center panel, exposing 9 panels
Source:	Appropriated text
Writer:	Leona F. Cordery
Printer:	Claire Rau
Binder:	Claire Rau
Holdings:	New York Public Library, Vassar College, Indiana University (Bloomington), Brown University, Rochester Institute of Technology, University of Delaware, Virginia Commonwealth University, Yale University
Subject:	Subject: Artists' books—Specimens

Illustration for page 105:

WOMEN'S STUDIO WORKSHOP ARTIST'S BOOK DETAILS

Title:	How to eat your enemy
Creator:	Claire Rau
Description:	How to Eat Your Enemy is based on a 14th century Richard Coeur de Lion crusading manuscript and the infamous card deck from the Iraq war. Portraits of terrorists from the FBI Most Wanted Terrorist web site stare at the reader, while the recto side recounts King Richard's apparent taste for the enemy flesh.
Paging:	[17] p.
Dimensions:	69 x 70 cm, folded to 23 x 22.5 cm.
Date:	2006
Publisher:	Women's Studio Workshop
Copyright Owner:	Claire Rau
Edition:	25
ISBN:	1893125491
Printing Method:	Letterpress, Screenprint
Binding:	Handmade slipcase
Structure:	Fold book
Typeface:	Caslon
Paper:	Arches 88
Funding Source:	New York State Council on the Arts
Other Notes:	Text translated and derived from 14th century manuscript by Leona F. Cordery
Other Notes:	3 bi-fold panels hinged to center panel, exposing 9 panels
Source:	Appropriated text
Writer:	Leona F. Cordery
Printer:	Claire Rau
Binder:	Claire Rau
Holdings:	New York Public Library, Vassar College, Indiana University (Bloomington), Brown University, Rochester Institute of Technology, University of Delaware, Virginia Commonwealth University, Yale University
Subject:	Subject: Artists' books—Specimens

Students, researchers, and collectors of artists' books who visit the Workshop web site will be lead to the artists' books archive search page. One may browse the entire collection or choose from numerous customized search boxes to retrieve the desired results. Search options include: keyword, creator, title, holdings, structure, binding, funding source, printing process, year, and print status. Because use of a controlled vocabulary greatly enhances successful searching, consistent terms have been used wherever possible to describe the various elements of the artists' books. A glossary containing an alphabetical listing of terms and their definitions accompanies the search boxes for structure, binding, and printing process. As additional terms are defined they are added to these user guides. When one or more title is retrieved via a search, the resulting screen display includes a thumbnail image of the artist's book cover, accompanied by the title, artist's name, date, and print status. If the title is still in print, a price is also displayed. Searchers may then click on the cover image, which will lead to a screen displaying additional thumbnail images of sample pages and the artist's description. Placing the cursor over one of these images will retrieve a larger browsing display. From this same screen one may click on "more info" to retrieve the public display of the database elements. (See sample illustration) Clicking on "PDF of book" allows the searcher to view or save the entire book file. An option to purchase the published artist's book is also offered on this same screen.

Future plans for improvements of the artists' book archive reflect advances in technology that enhance digital display and searching. Visitors to the archive search pages will discover a greatly enhanced visual experience when perusing the digitized artists' books. Implementation is currently underway to integrate a page-turning software into the archive so reading the standard codex will mimic tangible reading activity. For a great number of artists' books more sophisticated digital displays are necessary to capture the sculptural and structural details. A transition to streaming video for select books will offer a superior view of the movable and unique features with this technology. My goal to expose the metadata in this database to a much greater audience will be realized when the infrastructure is in place to map the elements to Dublin Core, a metadata standard. By making this database open access-compliant its content will become freely available and easily searchable by anyone. All of these initiatives will keep the Women's Studio Workshop artists' books archive vibrant and vital for current and future book artists and those who study and admire their work.

SYLVIA TURCHYN HEADS THE DEPARTMENT OF WESTERN EUROPEAN CATALOGUING AT INDIANA UNIVERSITY BLOOMINGTON, AND HAS CATALOGUED ALL OF THE ARTISTS' BOOKS PRODUCED BY THE WOMEN'S STUDIO WORKSHOP FOR THEIR WEBSITE.

BOOK ARTS IN THE CURRICULUM:

A COMMUNAL EFFORT

DAWN MCCUSKER I was first introduced to Women's Studio Workshop in 2006 when the director of the School of Art and Art History at James Madison University told the faculty about an opportunity to apply for WSW's artist's book residency. As a traditional graphic designer for fifteen years, I felt it necessary to explore the unique communication vehicle of an artist's book. I had mastered traditional book design with a process and production consisting of a digital file sent to some far-away printer, but the hands-on approach was an element I missed in contemporary graphic design.

After completing the residency in 2007, I was hooked. My experience at the Workshop was profoundly transformative, changing how I approach graphic design in practice and education. In the fall of 2007, I began taking steps to develop Book Arts education at the university.

In a time when most art and design schools are spread thin with the growing needs of students and faculty, why would James Madison add another concentration to our curriculum? The answer is that Book Arts is already inherent in a school that's engaged in a multi-disciplinary approach. The Bachelor of Fine Arts degree requires students to be as multifaceted as possible within their studio art education. The category of artists' books describes a production of printed or one-of-a-kind handmade books made by artists as artworks. This allows the student to challenge the traditional definition of a book. The realization that a book can move away from a traditional vessel that houses content into a sculptural object that challenges and engages its audience through the unique choice of structure, paper selection, and multiple processes is a new and exciting revelation.

Part of this school's engagement began in 2008, when the Women's Studio Workshop was invited to James Madison as one of our Dorothy Liskey Wampler Eminent Art Professorship recipients. Events included an exhibition of WSW artists' books in Sawhill Gallery, a lecture on the Workshop's thirty-four year history by co-founders Ann Kalmbach and Tatana Kellner, studio critiques, and a one-day workshop in papermaking. With WSW's assistance, we continued the development of our collection of artists' books in the Carrier Library. The library made its first purchase of WSW artists' books and has continued purchasing every year.

The collection of artists' books at James Madison has become a staple on the syllabi of many faculty members, who use it as a support for established and new curricula. As we continue to grow the collection, the selection process is varied to meet the needs of all faculty in the school. Since the inception, I have worked closely with the Special Collections liaison to select the artists' books. Variations I look for can be material, or structural, or based on final process choices including use of letterpress, silkscreen, photography, and papermaking.

For students, personally handling the books is an invaluable learning experience. Students, who are allowed to spend as much time as needed interacting with the collection, are surprised at the varying structures of the artists' book as well as the variety of media used to develop type and image. The following are examples of several studio art concentrations examining the art of the book.

Each semester, Corinne Diop, Professor of Art in photography, brings her *Digital Photography* class to view WSW and other artists' books in Special Collections. The assignment, "Hi Tech/ Lo Tech", includes an option for students to produce a handmade artist's book. If the student chooses this option, the juxtaposition occurs between the digital photography (hi tech), and the hand-constructed book (lo tech). Even if this option is not chosen, many students make a book for their final portfolio.

Professor Leslie Bellavance, Director of the School of Art and Art History, utilizes the collection in her art history course, *Topics in Twentieth Century Art: Contemporary Women Artists*. The assignment, "Scavenger Hunt: Artists' Books by Women Artists", requires the student to review the books produced by the Women's Studio Workshop. Students familiarize themselves with the form and content of artists' books and choose one book by a woman artist on which they write a three-page critical essay. Students in this course spend between two to five hours at the library reviewing the books.

The assignment to review five books and write an essay about one is similar to other writing assignments in the class, which require students to write about artworks that they could see in person. The difference is that the students' experience of the artists' books, as they expressed it in the essays, is at a more intimate level. Students more often discuss the artwork in terms of how it touched them personally or related to their own life experiences. Professor Bellavance states, "I have concluded that having more assignments incorporating artists' books earlier on in the semester will help students connect to the content and ideas of the artworks covered on a personal level."

As a graphic design educator, I see tangible benefits to exposing our students to fine art areas including artists' books. Bookmaking skills can only be a positive attribute for their final portfolios. The addition of hands-on learning provides a potential employer with a snapshot of the student's process, craft, and attention to detail; a computer can't build a mock-up for the client.

Artists' books in the graphic design curriculum are taught every other year in a course titled *Book Design* and sporadically in other design courses, depending on the instructor's goals. For example, my intermediate typography course developed an artist's book using a story chosen from *Invisible Cities* by Italo Calvino. I took the class to Special Collections to show them that the traditional definition of a book can take on a whole new meaning when interpreted by different artists. Artists' books offer the design student a personal and tactile connection to the design and a commitment to the execution of concept. With a hands-on project, the student becomes fully and physically invested in the piece, taking complete responsibility for its outcome. This gives a sense of pride and ownership in the work with an attention to detail and craft and a respect for materials and methods.

How is this different from any other design project? Concept is a constant in all coursework; however by following the production from start to finish the attributes become apparent because they are seeing the process unfold before them and not on a computer screen. Problems that are encountered with hands-on projects must be addressed in a thoughtful manner and resolved during the production. The blame for a negative outcome does not fall on a copy center or lack of software, it falls on them.

Although developing a new program at a university can be a slow process, we have all the tools we need—equipment and scholarly—to run an enriching Book Arts curriculum. We have purchased equipment to continue strengthening the development of the books, such as a book press and guillotine. I have a letterpress studio in my garage where I teach art and design students during the summer session. The summer 2010 letterpress students worked on a collaborative artists' book that was produced in the fall. The Graphic Design curriculum will offer *Book Design* every year instead of every two years. And finally, we are finding a permanent home for our papermaking equipment. The communal effort is strong and the benefit to the students' education is clear. The enthusiasm from students and faculty is unanimous—they just can't get enough!

DAWN MCCUSKER IS AN ASSOCIATE PROFESSOR OF GRAPHIC DESIGN AT JAMES MADISON UNIVERSITY AND IS ALSO #1 PRESS GIRL AT HER HOME STUDIO, PRESS GIRL PRESS.

THE CONFLUENCE OF WRITING

AND THE ARTISTS' BOOK

SUSAN VIGUERS

The difference between writing in a book of literature and in an artist's book is that in the latter the visual is a primary component of meaning. In a book of poetry, visually where a line begins and ends is important for meaning. In an artist's book that may also be true of text, but beyond that, the relationship of the writing to the page (which frequently includes imagery), and to the temporal and three-dimensional form of the book, and often even its graphic presence are all essential. Text in an artist's book is never an invisible vessel for semantic content.

Writing can exist in artists' books as just the opposite—as image, alluding to or evoking text, with little or no semantic content. Sometimes it literally cannot be read. In Tatana Kellner's B-11226: Fifty Years of Silence the handwritten Czech is indecipherable to most readers, but it is important in evoking an authentic personal story. In Susan Baker's Don't Bug the Waitress the never-ending monologue to which "the bore" subjects his victims at the next table degenerates into scrawl marks.

Other times text is an element in the imagery, as in the maps and diagrams in the visual cacophony of Heather O'Hara's The Handbook of Practical Geographies, existing to complete the image, at times to focus it, but it need not be read in total. In April Katz's Marking Time: Her Days much of the text is a facsimile of her mother's date book entries. Again, the handwriting and the context of the calendar are more important than reading all the words, though reading some is important. In Angela Jann and Emily Panzeri's Deus ex Machina handwriting provides the image background for the printed text pages. It echoes that text, picking up words or phrases, but much of it is illegible. "In the new art you often do NOT need to read the whole book," declares Ulises Carrión in his often quoted manifesto, "The New Art of Making Books."

There are many artists who are fascinated by visual forms (personal and media) of language: the personal recounting, the date book, the dictionary in Rita Mac-Donald's Family. Judith Mohns in Remembrance reproduces an obituary page from the August 26, 2001 edition of The New York Times, each iteration with most of the text made lighter or eliminated and a different type of word or phrase prominent—the various words for "die," name, age, birth information, occupation/

defining identity (homemaker, husband), and so forth—communicating in the process the sadness, the impossible weight and loss, of the everyday occurrence of the death of ordinary people. The interest in the graphic marks that make up a book of literature led Heidi Neilson to focus on an extra-textual element of writing, punctuation. Her *Atlas of Punctuation* is a rendering of fourteen texts, from Gaston Bachelard's *The Poetics of Space* to Dr. Seuss's *Horton Hears a Who* to Virginia Woolf's *To the Lighthouse*, for each book one page on which all the end punctuation marks of the book have been conflated. The name of each classic is important, necessary to focus our "reading." What we have is a non-verbal interpretation of text, visual insight into semantic meaning.

The semantic content of writing can also be important in artists' books, but that content is inseparable from its visual presence. In Katherine Aoki's *How I Lost My Vegetarianism* the graphic presence of the text, hand-carved print, which participates in and connects it to the linoleum block print illustrations, makes us read the text through a humorous, informal, primitive prism. Similarly, in Heather O'Hara's *The Handbook of Practical Geographies* the primary text and much of the imagery are both woodcut, giving the text the same weight and presence as that of the imagery. They are entwined, one giving focus to the other. The text is from a 1965 social studies textbook, *Geography and World Affairs*, and the imagery is collage (woodcut, digital, and screen printed), shifting in size and orientation, of politicians, dictators, presidents, people in the news, animal photographs, icons like the U.S. flag, ads, maps. The table of contents functions as the key to the satiric envisioning—"Oiling the Machine: the Gulf War" and "Welfare=Wealth+Warfare: the Philippines" are the first two chapters—in which text and image are fused.

Even when writing in its brevity and graphic simplicity does not call attention to itself visually, there is an infinite number of ways it can be a core participant in the creation of meaning that makes up an artist's book. In Katie Baldwin's *Treasure* the text works as a modality that is quite different from the imagery. The text is ostensibly what the book is about: a minimal story of a woman who renames herself "Treasure," a slightly adolescent and comic assertion of self-worth, and goes on a journey involving change and discovery, ominous in part. The imagery (the directions for a Japanese product of Jiffy Popcorn) comically undercuts and at the same time extends the significance of the text. What they have in common is travel by air, fire, change. The directions for popping Jiffy Popcorn follow a clear linear path (even without being able to read the Japanese text) and reinforces a forward movement to the primary (English) text, but there is a disjunction in the images on the page spreads that echoes the mysterious, nonsensical ellipses of that text. Images that bleed off one page edge are not completed on the next page, although the structure of the accordion sets up that expectation. The book's story, dominated by the text, is made up of moments, but exactly how one leads to the next is not as clear as simply the shape of a story, that of a central character, whose journey is both physical and psychological, to a land that is both a new home and dangerous. The image of the popcorn on the burner is at one moment domestic (we see a hand holding a pan) and at another dangerous (the popcorn on the fire suggesting a volcano). The brilliant orange that appears sparingly, but dramatically, primarily in the images of the stove burner, arrows, and, most significantly, large numbers (the steps in the directions) and, finally, the popped popcorn, paces and moves forward the narrative, a strange story, domestic and political, a meditation and an adventure. The text and image in one sense are quite separate, but it is the two together that create the book.

When reading a standard text, one quickly forgets its physical presence and conjures up meaning separate from the graphic marks. That does not necessarily characterize writing in artists' books, but at times it does, in spite of the graphic importance of the text and its relationship to image and structure. Tatana Kellner's *B-11226: Fifty Years of Silence* is one such book. The imagery, renderings of family photographs against the wall of names in Prague's Pinkas Synagogue and photographs of the concentration camps, give context to the text. The handwritten Czech text on every other verso page also functions for an English speaker as imagery. But the core of the book is the printed text, the artist's father's understated, factual, horrific account of his Holocaust concentration camp experience. A paper cast of her father's arm tattooed with his concentration camp number is always present as one reads, at times even awkwardly interrupting the flow of the words, but the world that is conjured up by the language is at the heart of the book.

In Lori Spencer's *Shared Memories* the writing is also the center of the book: narrative moments in the growing up of two sisters, and their relationship, exist in and through the verbal story telling. But the visual and the structural define our understanding of that story. Graphically, the two sisters' versions of each incident are presented each in its own typeface on the two sides of a pop-up that crosses the gutter, thus making them slope away from each other, embodying the mutual exclusivity of perspective. The page spreads alternate between imagery and text. When it is imagery, the center image, structurally positioned so that the two pages fall around it, is a constant, that of the two children. When the page spread is verbal, present-day reflections on the incident surround the central pop-up story. The book's physical structure enacts and functions as a metaphoric context for the narrative, which is primarily rendered in the form of text.

Susan E. King's *Women and Cars* is the story of a woman and her two aunts and their cars, augmented by quotations from various books (Nancy Drew stories, *The Autobiography of Alice B. Toklas* and others), all of which invert the traditional association of the automobile with men, feminizing it. This is a flag book and the text is fragmented into blocks, printed on one side of the flag "pages." That fragmentation undermines clear narrative sequencing, focusing our attention on the theme itself, women and cars. The flag book is a dramatic structure transforming itself when opened fully. Appropriately at that point the reader sees only an image of a young woman in front of her car, the image metaphorically subsuming the text.

Maureen Cummins' *The Business Is Suffering* is a reminder of one of the problems inherent in displaying many artists' books, even when multiple spreads are shown. *The Business Is Suffering* looks like a ledger book. Along the case spine, we read: RHD & Bro; Richmond, VA; Dealers & Auctioneers; Letters 1846-1863. On the verso of each page is a facsimile of part of a correspondence of the slave trading firm R.H. Dickinson & Brothers—an address, a date, names, a postmark—behind an image of the cargo hold of a slave ship. This image appears on each verso, but gradually the number of human figures is reduced to one and then none. On each recto is a different letter, printed over a facsimile of the original handwritten one. Text functions so strongly as image that one might assume it is necessary only to dip into reading the printed text to feel the book's power. That is misleading; absorbing all the text is necessary to experience fully the bitter, complex, tragic understanding of the artist's rendering of humans reduced to salable produce.

SUSAN VIGUERS, A BOOK ARTIST AND WRITER, IS PROFESSOR AND DIRECTOR OF THE MFA BOOK ARTS/ PRINTMAKING PROGRAM AT THE UNIVERSITY OF THE ARTS IN PHILADELPHIA.
Ulises Carrión in his "The New Art of Making Books" declares, "The writer of the new art writes very little or does not write at all." That, indeed, can be true. Many artists' books, however, are hybrid works in which the verbal not only has a visual presence, participating in both the two- and three-dimensional spaces that make up a book, but also functions as writing that, as in a book of literature, must be read. In terms of a viewer's reception, there may be a momentary disjuncture between reading the visual and absorbing semantic content, but the two can exist together in an audience's experience of powerful works of arts.

EXHIBITION CHECKLIST

HAND

The Complex of All These
Abigail Uhteg
14" x 11"
Etching and letterpress
2009 Edition of 35

Eight Breakfasts in 8 Pages
Deborah Frederick
7.25" x 9.75"
Silkscreen
1999 Edition of 100

Everyday Road Signs
Carol Barton
7.5" x 8.75"
Silkscreen and die cut
1988 Edition of 70

First Visit
Sara Langworthy
8.75" x 7.25"
Photocopy
2001 Edition of 40

Headdress
Ann Kalmbach and
Tatana Kellner
5.75" x 11.75"
Silkscreen
1983 Edition of 75

How I Lost My Vegetarianism
Katherine Aoki
8" x 9.75"
Relief print
1998 Edition of 100

How to Eat Your Enemy
Claire Rau
9" x 9"
Silkscreen and letterpress
2006 Edition of 25

Patterned Pleasures
Amanda Kalinoski
7.5" x 5.25"
Silkscreen and letterpress
2009 Edition of 50

*Handbook of Practical
Geographies*
Heather O'Hara
11" x 17"
Silkscreen, linocut, digital
2004 Edition of 100

Relation
Ann Lovett
6.5" x 3.75"
Offset
1999 Edition of 200

Ruderal Plants in Manhattan
Susan Mills
5" x 4.75"
Silkscreen
1995 Edition of 100

Skim Milk and Soft Wax
Dani Leventhal
12.5" x 9.75"
Silkscreen, intaglio, digital
and die cut
2008 Edition of 36

Treasure
Katie Baldwin
8" x 8"
Moku hanga, letterpress
and silkscreen
2008 Edition of 35

Truly Bone
Karen Kunc
8" x 7.5"
Intaglio, letterpress
1998 Edition of 50

VOICE

Bird Watching
Paula McCartney
10" x 8"
Chromogenic and
digital prints
2006 Edition of 40

Crazy Quilt
Maureen Cummins
10" x 10"
Silkscreen and letterpress
1998 Edition of 100

Don't Bug the Waitress
Susan Baker
11.5" x 7"
Silkscreen
1987 Edition of 200

Errors of the Amanuensis
Ann Kalmbach and
Tatana Kellner
8.5" x 10.75"
Letterpress
2010 Edition of 30

Forgotten Knowledge
Marisol Limon Martinez
7.75" x 11.125"
Silkscreen and photocopy
2002 Edition of 50

Lucha por la Vida
Ral Veroni
6" x 8.5"
Silkscreen and digital
2000 Edition of 40

Momotaro/Peach Boy
Tomie Arai
15.5" x 11.5"
Intaglio and letterpress
2003 Edition of 25

None of Your Damn Business
Barbara Leoff Burge
9.125" x 7.75"
Silkscreen
2010 Edition of 50

Pistol/Pistil: Botanical Ballistics
Ann Kalmbach and
Tatana Kellner
8.75" x 6.75"
Silkscreen
1997 Edition of 100

Remembrance
Judith Mohns
6.5" x 6.5"
Digital and offset
2003 Edition of 400

Scattered Memory
Edie Tsong
12" x 6.25"
Silkscreen and letterpress
2005 Edition of 50

Transatlantic Balderdash
Ann Kalmbach and
Tatana Kellner
6.75" x 12"
Letterpress, silkscreen, digital
2010 Edition of 25

Unfolding Architecture
Emily Speed
8" x 3.5"
Silkscreen and letterpress
2007 Edition of 90

*What's Happening with
Momma?*
Clarissa Sligh
11.5" x 6.25"
Silkscreen and letterpress
1988 Edition of 150

Women and Cars
Susan Elizabeth King
8.125" x 5.75"
Offset
1983 Edition of 500

VISION

4X4
Barbara Leoff Burge,
Ann Kalmbach, Tatana
Kellner and Anita Wetzel
7.5" x 6.75"
Silkscreen, letterpress and
handmade paper
1981 Edition of 100

Atlas of Punctuation
Heidi Neilson
9.75" x 8.5"
Letterpress
2004 Edition of 100

The Business Is Suffering
Maureen Cummins
13" x 9.5"
Silkscreen and letterpress
2003 Edition of 50

Empress Bullet
Louise Odes Neaderland
8.5" x 9.5"
Offset
1982 Edition of 100

*71125: Fifty Years of Silence,
Eva Kellner's Story*
Tatana Kellner
12" x 20"
Silkscreen, die cut, and
handmade paper
1992 Edition of 40

*B-11226: Fifty Years of
Silence, Eugene Kellner's Story*
Tatana Kellner
12" x 20"
Silkscreen, die cut and
handmade paper
1992 Edition of 50

The House with Four Walls
Zarina
16.5" x 29.5"
Intaglio and letterpress
1991 Edition of 25

A Nuclear Atlas
Sharon Gilbert
11.5" x 9.5"
Offset
1982 Edition of 500

Seven Lady Saintes
Erica Van Horn
9.5" x 8"
Silkscreen
1985 Edition of 90

Site Readings
Anne George
7.5" x 4.5"
Offset
1993 Edition of 225

*What Day Is It?
An Artist's Book*
Kate Van Houten
9.75" x 11.25"
Silkscreen
1986 Edition of 63

Wrongly Bodied Two
Clarissa Sligh
10" x 7.25"
Silkscreen and digital
2004 Edition of 46

INDEX

ARTISTS WHO PUBLISHED BOOKS

AT WOMEN'S STUDIO WORKSHOP

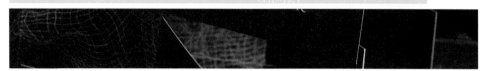

Judith Anderson
Katherine Aoki
Tomie Arai
Lynne Avadenka
Susan Baker
Katie Baldwin
Molly Barker
Mariona Barkus
Carol June Barton
J. Catherine Bebout
Margarita Becerra Cano
Joshua Saul Beckman
Miriam Beerman
Barbara Beisinghoff
Meg Belichick
Roberley Bell
Elisabeth Belliveau
Suzanne Benton
Judith Blumberg
Sue Bucholz
Barbara Leoff Burge
Nancy Callahan
Carissa Carman
Nancy Chalker-Tennant
Irene Chan
Wei Jane Chir
Amy Ciullo
Libby Clarke
Beatrice Conover
Lisa Cooper
Stephanie Copoulos-Selle
Maureen Cummins
Sara Cushing
Terry Lee Czechowski
M. J. Davison
Daniela Deeg
Nancy W. Diessner
Stacy Doris
Mindell Dubansky
Eve Faulkes

Ana Fernandez
Kate Ferrucci
Rachel Frank
Lorrie Frear
Deborah Frederick
Ellie Ga
Annette Gates
Cheri Gaulke
Anne George
Rimma Gerlovina
April Gertler
Anne Gorrick
Sharon Gilbert
Jennifer Grimyser
Dawn Hachenski McCusker
Erica Harris
William Harroff
Mei-ling Hom
Gretchen Hooker
Judith Hoyt
Hawley Hussey
Katherine Immonen
Jahjehan Bath Ives
Diane Jacobs
Angela Jann
Linda Johnson
Amanda Kalinoski
Ann Kalmbach
Rochelle Kaplan Rubenstein
Kake Art
Michael Kasper
April Katz
Tatana Kellner
Ann Marie Kennedy
Melinda Kennedy
Susan Elizabeth King
Louise Krasniewicz
Janis Krasnow
Ann M. Kresge
Ellen Kucera
Karen S. Kunc

Sara Langworthy
Barbara Leoff Burge
Danielle Leventhal
Kristy Lewis
Marisol Limon Martinez
Cynthia Lollis
Erika Lopez
Angela Lorenz
Ann Lovett
Rebecca Lown
Rita MacDonald
Eva Mantell
Judith Cohen Margolis
Valerie Maynard
Paula McCartney
Nora Lee McGillivray
Susan Mills
Judith Mohns
Linda Montano
Lois Morrison
Colleen Mullins
Louise Odes Neaderland
Heidi Neilson
Beverly L. Nichols
Baco Ohama
Heather O'Hara
Emily Panzeri
Quimetta Perle
Sarah Peters
Lyman Piersma
Claire Rau
Hilda Raz
Leslie Roitman
Sandra Rowe
Akiko Sakaizumi
Alyce Santoro
Jenny Sapora
Amy Schmierbach
Terry Schupbach-Gordon
Gary Schwartz
Sandra Schwimmer

Patricia Scobey
Christina Seely
Miriam Shenitzer
Barbara Siegel
Clarissa Sligh
Melissa Smedley
Jenny R. Snider
T. Ellen Sollod
Indigo Som
Karen Spears
Emily Speed
Lori Spencer
Sarah Stengle
Carolyn Swiszcz
Hannah Taylor
Amanda Thackray
Cynthia Thompson
Lisa Titus
Edie Tsong
Sandra Turley
Patty Tyrol
Abigail Uhteg
Erica Van Horn
Kate Van Houten
Ral Veroni
Beata Veszely
Susan Viguers
Ellen Wallenstein
Bisa Washington
Anita Wetzel
Jody Williams
Amy Wilson
Tona Wilson
Patricia Wilson-Adams
Cynthia Winika
Paul Woodbine
Melinda Yale
Liz Zanis
Emna Zghal
Zarina

gro since I left Richmond. I have
mers Bank to hold up my draft a
g I may yet hold enough to pay.
$258. This is to inform you that
nt nd. I shall pay it as soon as I

Wilmington the next week if they
ll remove them down in Chowan

ACKNOWLEDGEMENTS

I hope he nor you will abuse me

ours in haste
J Williams

Women's Studio Workshop would like to express deep appreciation and thanks to Kathleen Walkup, the curator of this exhibition, whose tremendous efforts, unflagging energy and dedication over two years have brought this exhibition to fruition. We also want to acknowledge and thank Elizabeth Fischbach for bringing her expertise to the exhibition design and working tirelessly with Kathleen and the WSW staff over the past year. WSW also extends thanks to the many colleagues who have offered insightful contributions to the exhibition catalogue.

WSW is honored to have this opportunity to present our artists' books at the Grolier Club. Our thanks and appreciation to Dr. Robert J. Ruben of the Grolier Club who has been a wonderful supporter of WSW's publishing program and facilitated WSW in its exhibition proposal to the Grolier Club. Many thanks to the Grolier Club staff for their support, in particular Eric Holzenberg, Director, and Megan Smith, Exhibition Coordinator.

We are especially grateful to Dawn McCusker for her superb catalogue design. The printing of the catalogue was made possible with support from The Cowles Charitable Trust and Vassar College Library. Additionally we would like to acknowledge Gary Gray of Lithography by Design for his excellent printing and guidance throughout the design process.

WSW's artists' books publishing program has been made possible by the generous support of many people and institutions. Artists' Books residencies have been funded by New York State Council on the Arts, the National Endowment for the Arts, Mid Atlantic Arts Foundation, Milton & Sally Avery Arts Foundation, Ora Schneider Residency Grant and The Andy Warhol Foundation for the Visual Arts. Our goal of getting the work into the public domain is made possible through sales of the books to libraries and educational institutions across the country. We would like to applaud the visionary support of six repositories committed to acquiring every past and future WSW edition: Vassar College Library, Yale University Library, Rochester Institute of Technology, Indiana University Bloomington, University of Delaware and Virginia Commonwealth University.

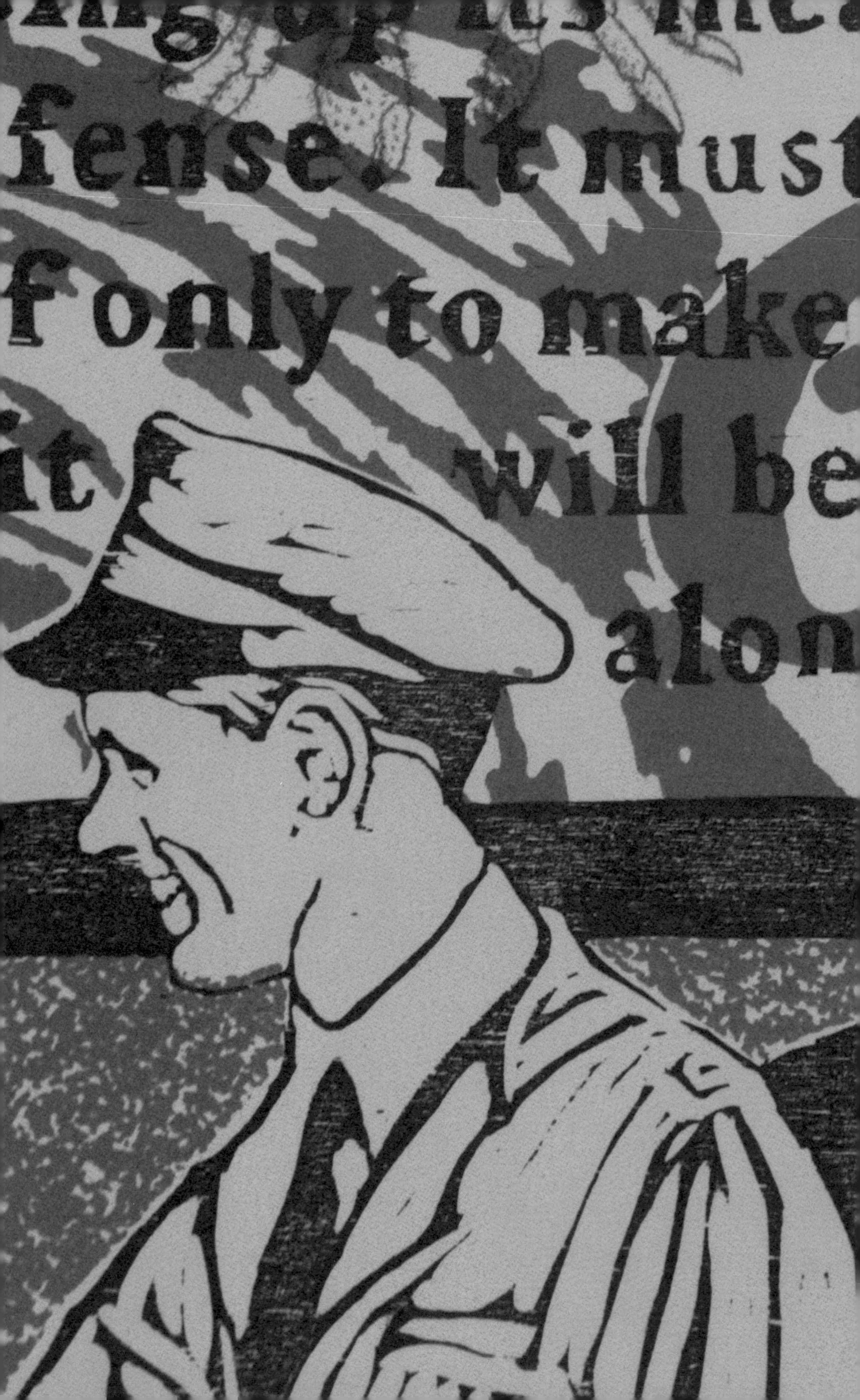
fense. It must
fonly to make
it will be
alon